SCIENCE IN CINEMA

Teaching Science Fact
Through Science Fiction Films

SCIENCE IN CINEMA

Teaching Science Fact
Through Science Fiction Films

LEROY W. DUBECK
SUZANNE E. MOSHIER
JUDITH E. BOSS

TEACHERS COLLEGE PRESS

Teachers College, Columbia University
New York and London

Published by Teachers College Press, 1234 Amsterdam Avenue,
New York, NY 10027

Paperback cover photo: "2001: A SPACE ODYSSEY" © 1968 Metro-Goldwyn-Mayer Inc.,
color, 139 minutes.
Producer/Director, Stanley Kubrick; Screenplay by Stanley Kubrick and Arthur C. Clarke;
Special Effects designed and directed by Stanley Kubrick, for which he won an Academy
Award.

Library of Congress Cataloging-in-Publication Data

Dubeck, Leroy W., 1939–

　Science in cinema.

　Bibliography: p.
　Includes index.
　1. Science — Study and teaching (Secondary) —
Audio-visual aids.   2. Science fiction films — History
and criticism.   3. Motion pictures in science.
I. Moshier, Suzanne E.   II. Boss, Judith E.   III. Title.
Q192.D8   1988　　　507′.12　　　88-8575

ISBN 0-8077-2916-7
ISBN 0-8077-2915-9 (pbk.)

Manufactured in the United States of America

93　92　91　90　89　88　　　1　2　3　4　5　6

Contents

Acknowledgments

The authors wish to thank Dr. Joseph Schmuckler, professor of chemistry and science education at Temple University, for invaluable assistance in writing this book. Also, the following research associates contributed to portions of nine chapters: Patricia Goerlich, John F. Hummel, Harrison C. Kornbau, Larry Melton, Bruce Thompson, and Joseph F. Zisk.

Jennifer Steinberg, David Grossman, and Katherine Cooper provided cast, credits, and distributors for the films.

Additional research support and manuscript typing were provided by Marjorie Huseman, Rose Tatlow, and Antoinette J. Dubeck. Leslie Alexander drew most of the illustrations.

The still photographs were provided by the Museum of Modern Art/Film Still Archives, courtesy of Allied Artists, Eagle Lion Films, Metro-Goldwyn-Mayer, Paramount Pictures, Twentieth Century-Fox, Universal Pictures, and Warner Brothers.

This material is based upon work supported by the National Science Foundation under grants MDR-8650104 and DPE-8320038. Any opinions, findings, conclusions, or recommendations expressed in this publication are those of the authors and do not necessarily reflect the views of the National Science Foundation.

Introduction

Educators have noted the decline in American science education since the post-Sputnik pinnacle and have urged its improvement.[1] In 1983 the National Science Board recommended that high school science courses cover fewer topics and pay more attention to "the integration of remaining facts, concepts, and principles within each discipline and with other sciences and areas such as mathematics, technology and the social sciences." The report also urged that precollege education prepare students "to participate intelligently as informed citizens in the transition from an industrialized society to a post-industrialized service and information age. . . . "[2] Thus, not pure science alone, but additionally knowledge of the uses and abuses of applied science received the board's recommendation for high school science courses.

Isolating knowledge of one science from that of another and from its application in other fields seemingly has turned the public to pseudoscience. The belief in a large variety of pseudosciences among college students is well documented,[3] and there is no reason to doubt that this interest begins before entering college. The causes are complex. One such cause is the failure of science to fulfill its early utopian promises. Instead of ending war or providing unlimited energy for the benefit of humanity, nuclear power is seen as having brought us the constant dread of annihilation or — even worse — a lingering life of constant and painful illness from radiation. Instead of curing all bodily ills, medical science has created antibiotic-resistant disease agents, disastrous side effects from wonder drugs, and biological warfare agents. Instead of bountiful harvests of insect-free agricultural products, chemistry has given us polluted fields, undrinkable water, acid rain, and "designer drugs" for the addict.

There are at least four other contributing factors. Politicians use "science" as their scapegoat, and the public blames scientists and their creations, instead of those who misused the knowledge and technology, for the adverse effects noted above. Imbalanced media presentations are a second cause. Pollution, nuclear accidents, and disasters of every sort make headlines; wild speculation and "interpretation" of scientific phenomena earn higher television ratings than simple facts; yet items like Gore-Tex, Thinsulate, a new strain of wheat, or another wonder drug seldom receive mention, let alone emphasis. They receive only commercial application. A third cause for the turn to pseudoscience is our culture's irrational belief in the "easy answer," the "quick fix": apply money, wait three days, and all problems will be solved. Or, in terms of knowledge, enter the educational system, put in time, and come out certified as educated. Fourth, the populace little realize that the "miracles of science" they hear about, use daily, dread, or anticipate, derive from fundamental scientific principles that must be learned before the "miracles" can be created. The well-known aphorism of astronomer and science fiction author Arthur C. Clarke is appropriate: "Any sufficiently advanced technology is indistinguishable from magic." Without knowledge of fundamental scientific principles, our technology is indistinguishable from magic and science is indistinguishable from pseudoscience or science fiction.

If science seems to many to have failed in the real world, it still offers hope and the fulfillment of dreams in science fiction. The popularity of *Star Wars, The Empire Strikes Back, Return of the Jedi, E.T.*, and numerous other science fiction or fantasy films is unprecedented. We have tried to tap the great attraction this form of "media magic" holds for young people and to use science fiction films as educational tools to build interest in and awareness of real science and its interaction with the world. We believe that, with appropriate supporting materials and science teachers trained in using this new technique, science fiction films can help reverse the negative attitudes that many students have toward real science by moving them from familiar experiences they enjoy to unfamiliar experiences they expect to be dull and difficult — like learning physics, astronomy, biology, and chemistry.

Our tool for achieving this is the use of science fiction films to enhance students' understanding of scientific principles by having them identify illustrations — and violations — of scientific principles portrayed in these films. This requires students to undertake critical analyses of the films by applying abstract scientific principles they have learned in the classroom. If they begin to do this with science fiction films, we believe they will transfer the technique to other experiences and be less likely to be taken in by the claims of pseudoscience in other formats, such as supermarket tabloids, TV commercials, and "news" stories.

In addition to learning specific scientific principles related to a given film and the principles of scientific analysis, students may also become interested in the relationships among science, technology, and society that are often portrayed in the films. They may also be interested in the relationships between the films and relevant literature.

DEVELOPMENT OF THIS TEXT

While there is little research on using science fiction films to teach science or to change students' attitudes toward science, the authors have had notably positive responses to this method. Dr. Leroy Dubeck, a physics professor at Temple University, has taught an introductory course using science fiction films to introduce students to science for a decade. Many students have stated that the course induced enough interest that they planned to enroll in additional science courses. Several of these students were teachers excited about the application of this approach to the precollege level.

Dr. Dubeck's description of this teaching strategy in the *Journal of College Science Teaching* elicited significant interest from college faculty wishing to introduce a similar course on their own campuses.[4] With the support of an NSF grant, Dr. Dubeck, in collaboration with Dr. Suzanne Moshier of the University of Nebraska at Omaha biology department, adapted the techniques of the college-level course, drafting a teachers' guide for using science fiction films in a ninth- or tenth-grade general science course. "Teaching Fact with Fiction"[5] describes the use of this technique at the precollege level.

During a two-week summer institute for gifted students at Temple University in July 1986, 24 ninth- and tenth-grade students screened science fiction films, with Drs. Dubeck and Moshier conducting one of the sessions. The students' evaluations and enthusiastic involvement in the morning-long discussion demonstrated their enjoyment of the film and the scientific principles related to it. But they were also interested in the societal issues raised by the film. Furthermore, the faculty involved with that institute were convinced that a great majority of the students would have liked to read and discuss relevant science fiction and other literature.

In 1986 Dr. Dubeck, in collaboration with Dr. Moshier and Dr. Judith Boss, of the English department at the University of Nebraska at Omaha, received another NSF grant to complete the teachers' study guide to the use of science fiction films at the pre-college level. The addition of Dr. Boss provided someone well-versed in science fiction literature, so that the study guide could provide access to the larger themes and relevant literature of the ten main films.

In 1987 Dr. Dubeck, in collaboration with Drs. Moshier and Boss, received another NSF grant, under which 24 precollege science teachers were trained to use science fiction films as a supplement to the regular science curriculum. The response thus far has been favorable.

JUSTIFICATION

Skeptics may ask whether it is worthwhile to screen an entire science fiction film for only a few minutes of science content. We believe that the screening of science fiction films may enhance the learning of science in several ways:

1. The actual scientific principles illustrated or violated in the films will be better understood by the students than if they were learned solely from more traditional approaches. Films directly visualize the abstract scientific principles in a manner easier for most students to understand than any mathematical formulation could provide. This is especially true for inexperienced science students, who often find it difficult to visualize the real applications of the subject studied. In short, films make the abstract concrete.

2. We have found that the hundreds of adult learners who have enrolled in the course Dr. Dubeck teaches at Temple University appear to learn scientific principles related to the film, but not actually illustrated in the film, better than they would in a typical introductory level science course. This is probably because of their enhanced interest in science generated by science fiction films.

3. Screening the films and discussing them appears to enhance the understanding of scientific processes and the relationship among science, technology, and society. This is critically important in helping students distinguish between scientific and pseudoscientific approaches to issues.

4. Students' attitudes toward science appear to become more positive. This motivation of students in science may be the single most important outcome of the use of science fiction films in precollege science classes.

In order to maximize the motivational impact of science fiction films on students, we suggest utilizing relevant science fiction and other literature. At the 1986 Temple University institute for gifted students mentioned above, most of the female students wanted to read additional literature related to the films. This is consistent with national trends in science fiction literature. Most readers of science fiction in the 1920s through the 1950s were male adolescents—an estimated 90% of the readership. Much of the science fiction literature of those days consisted of "hard science" stories, in which the "idea," as explained in a "scientist's" monologue, dominated plot and character development. This writing appealed to male adolescents (and might have to female adolescents as well, had their society not discouraged females from participating in intellectual activities).

Today, nearly half of science fiction readers are females of all ages, and science fiction stories currently published reflect the change in readership; fantasy and "soft science" stories have increased proportionally. In fact, more pure fantasy is published than traditional science fiction. In these stories, plot and character development are more important than an interesting scientific theme. These kinds of stories are often read by individuals with meager scientific backgrounds or by people who prefer their science integrated with — even subordinated to — social concerns. However, these individuals do have a latent interest in science that could be aroused by science fiction literature as well as science fiction films.

In its position paper, "Standards for the Preparation and Certification for Teachers of Science K–12," the National Science Teachers Association (NSTA) called for the training of all science teachers in the relationships among science, technology, and society; further, the NSTA report noted that when states increase science or mathematics requirements (as some are doing) "without modifying the content and teaching strategies to appeal to the interests and background of the majority of students the consequences are predictable: school dropout rates from ninth grade to graduation of 30%, a national disgrace."[6] Our experience has convinced us that using science fiction films and literature to teach science can motivate a far broader spectrum of students in science than can be motivated by traditional methods.

USING THIS TEXT

This text is designed so that it can be used for an entire course. We have provided thorough analyses of ten films and the scientific principles they illustrate as well as the relevant literature. In addition, we have provided briefer analyses of 24 other films and appropriate scientific commentary.

We recommend, however, that a teacher use the material in this text to enrich a traditional science course rather than to supplant it, and we recommend using three or four science fiction films per semester. We further recommend that teachers use the text as an illustration of how such films and literature may be incorporated into a science course.

Refer to the contents for the films included in the book and to the index for the scientific topics discussed in the various chapters. Each of the first ten chapters of this book treats a single film, providing information on credits and distributors; a plot summary; discussion of the scientific principles related to the film; scientific commentary that follows the film's sequence of events and is highlighted by subject headings; classroom activities (exercises and discussion topics); literary commentary on the sources for the film; and bibliographic information. Chapter 11 includes abbreviated information on 24 additional films—credits, plot summary, and sequential scientific commentary. (Note that all of the 24 additional films are available on videocassette except *Crack in the World*.)

The films themselves may be incorporated into science courses in a number of ways, depending upon equipment resources, budgets, length of class periods, and schedule flexibility. Taking these variables into account, we have devised the following three major strategies:

1. The film could be screened in its entirety on two or more consecutive days during the normal class period, using either a videocassette recorder or a 16-mm projector. Since the films vary in length from 81 minutes to 130 minutes, and a typical secondary school class period is 45–50 minutes, it will take two or even three class periods to screen an entire film. The advantages of this mode are that it avoids any scheduling problems for the students in seeing the films and that it requires the school to have only one copy of the film. The disadvantages are that at least two class periods will be consumed in screening the film and that there may be a slight reduction in plot continuity.

2. The film could be screened in its entirety at one showing in school. This may be done by combining a regular class period with a lunch or study period preceding or following it, by using a class period at the end of the day and asking the students to remain for an extra 45 minutes or so, or by screening the entire picture at the end of the regular class day. Here the advantage is plot continuity, while the disadvantage is scheduling. This mode also requires only one copy of the film.

3. The third alternative is to use VCRs to allow the students individually to screen the film in its entirety either in the school or at home. Within the next few years, virtually all secondary schools will have at least some VCRs for students to use during study periods or after school hours. By the end of 1986, over 40 million American homes possessed VCRs,[7] and projections estimate that 90% of all households will have a VCR by the early to mid 1990s.[8] The advantage of using VCRs to screen films outside of class is that no class time is used to watch the entire film, although the teacher may replay brief portions on a classroom VCR to discuss particular scientific principles or sociological aspects of a given film. In addition, students will be able to replay portions a number of times to better understand the scientific principles illustrated or violated.

The disadvantage to this mode is that students without a VCR at home must have access to one at school. In addition, the school will have to buy a number of copies of a given film. For example, four copies would be needed to permit each student in a class of twenty to take a tape home overnight during a five-day period. However, four copies of a film on videotape typically costs less than one rental of a 16-mm film, and the school permanently owns the videotapes.

The strategies demonstrated here may be applied to lessons on different scientific principles or may be transferred to science fiction films not mentioned here — even to films not yet released. Topics we treat at length may be abbreviated, and topics we discuss briefly may be amplified. Using the material in this text as a guide, any precollege science teacher should be able to create his or her own lessons built upon science fiction films, television shows, or literature. (Additional resources on science fiction films and literature, as well as on the use of science fiction in teaching, may be found in the appropriate sections within the bibliography at the end of this book.) As a new approach to science teaching that works and increases motivation, the system we describe holds much promise, and we hope this text will be a source of inspiration and innovation as much as a collection of useful lessons.

NOTES

1. National Science Foundation, *What Are the Needs in the Pre-College Science, Mathematics, and Social Sciences? Views from the Field*, NSF SE (Washington, DC: National Science Foundation, 1983), pp. 80–89.

2. National Science Foundation, *Educating Americans for the 21st Century*, CPCE-NSF-03 (Washington, DC: National Science Foundation), pp. 98, 101.

3. Hoffmaster, S., "Pseudoscience — Teaching by Counterexample," *Journal of College Science Teaching* (1986): 432.

4. Dubeck, L. W., "Science and Science Fiction Films," *Journal of College Science Teaching* 11(1981): 111.

5. Dubeck, L. W., and S. E. Moshier, "Teaching Fact with Fiction," *American Educator* (Winter 1985): 41.

6. Aldridge, B. G., "Standards for the Preparation and Certification for Teachers of Science K–12," *NSTA Report* (October 1985): 7.

7. *Broadcasting Magazine* (13 June 1986): 188.

8. *Appliance* (July 1987): 14.

SCIENCE IN CINEMA

Teaching Science Fact
Through Science Fiction Films

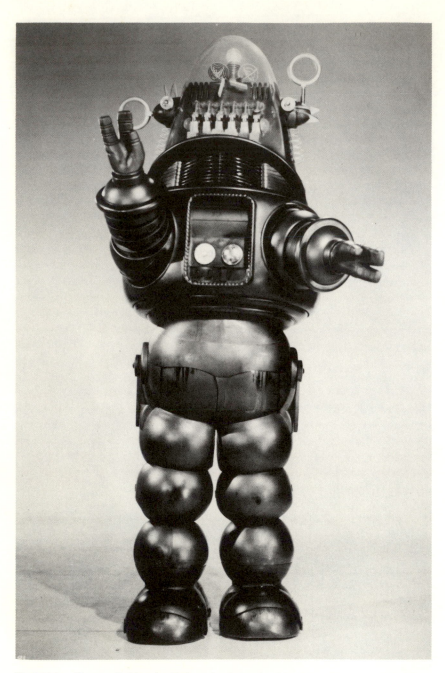

Forbidden Planet: Robby the Robot, built by Dr. Morbius using the advanced technology of the Krell. (Photo: Museum of Modern Art/Film Stills Archive. Courtesy of Metro-Goldwyn-Mayer.)

CHAPTER 1

Forbidden Planet

- MGM (USA), 1956, color, 98 minutes
- **Credits:** *Producer*, Nicholas Nayfack; *director*, Fred M. Wilcox; *story*, Irving Block and Allen Adler; *screenplay*, Cyril Hume; *cinematographer*, George Folsey; *special effects*, A. Arnold Gillespie, Warren Newscombe, Irving G. Ries, Joshua Meador; *music*, Louis and Bebe Barron
- **Cast:** Walter Pidgeon (Dr. Morbius), Anne Francis (Altaira), Leslie Nielson (Commander Adams), Warren Stevens (Dr. Ostrow), Jack Kelly (Lt. Farman), Earl Holliman (the cook), and Robby the Robot
- **Distributors:** *16 mm*—Films, Inc., 35 South West Street, Mt. Vernon, NY 10550, (800) 223-6246; *Videotape*—CBS Video, 1700 Broadway, New York, NY 10019

PLOT SUMMARY

In A.D. 2200 a rescue expedition from Earth arrives at Altair IV, a planet of the main sequence star Altair, to discover the fate of a prior expedition. The only survivors are a philologist, Dr. Morbius, and his daughter Altaira, nicknamed Alta. Dr. Morbius has constructed a remarkable robot, Robby, using the technology of the now-extinct race, the Krell. This superrace was ethically and technologically a million years in advance of the human race. In fact, they had previously traveled to Earth and brought back specimens of earthly animals that still survived on their planet. The Krell race had vanished in a single night some 200,000 years earlier, when they stood on the brink of their greatest technological achievement, according to Dr. Morbius. The rescue expedition is led by Commander Adams, who, along with the ship's physician, Dr. Ostrow, is given a guided tour by Dr. Morbius of a gigantic Krell machine. The machine occupies 8,000 cubic miles beneath the surface of the planet and is powered by 9,200 thermonuclear reactors. This gigantic machine has maintained itself over the 2,000 centuries since the Krell vanished.

Dr. Morbius tells his would-be rescuers that a mysterious monster killed all the members of the prior expedition except his wife and himself.

His wife died later of natural causes, after giving birth to his daughter. Morbius fears that the monster will return and urges his rescuers to leave.

Adams and Ostrow learn that Morbius has permanently increased his IQ by using a Krell machine that had been used to train Krell children. The machine allows the user to create a replica of any object being thought of; the object is recreated each microsecond. It uses as a power source the vast Krell thermonuclear furnace system. A series of dials along one of the walls in the laboratory measures the energy supplied by the Krell power plant. Each dial has a scale that is 10 times larger than the previous dial. As Morbius uses the Krell educational machine only the first dial registers the consumption of energy.

The rescue expedition is repeatedly attacked by the reactivated monster. Their weapons are useless against it. They eventually surmise that the monster is constantly being recreated every microsecond by the great Krell machine using the thermonuclear power plants. Dr. Ostrow takes a brain "boost" from the Krell educational machine and then explains the mystery before he dies. The Krell had achieved the independence of the body from material surroundings. Their great machine could convert any mental image of the Krell into actual material substance, using the vast power plant within it. But the Krell had forgotten that they too had a subconscious, including an id. "Monsters from the id" destroyed them.

Dr. Morbius's id is the source of the monster that killed all of his colleagues 20 years earlier and that now threatens to destroy both the rescue expedition and his own daughter, who has said that she wished to return to Earth with Commander Adams, whom she loves. Nothing can stop the monster, and the film portrays the use of vast amounts of energy as row after row of dials are lighted by the power being consumed by the Krell machine, which is creating the monster. Dr. Morbius orders Robby to kill the monster, but a built-in injunction against killing any intelligent being paralyzes the robot because it knows that the monster originates in Dr. Morbius's own subconscious. At last, when Morbius realizes the truth, he renounces this creature, but the mental effort kills him. As he lays dying he asks Commander Adams to throw a switch and then tells him that this has activated a chain reaction that will destroy the planet in 24 hours. The rescue party, Altaira, and Robby escape in the nick of time.

Special Effects.   The model work is outstanding. The spaceship and the robot sequences are truly extraordinary for 1956. There is moderate matte work, and the backgrounds, with fine studio-crafted interiors, are exceptional. The film is a forerunner of the later *2001* and the "Star Trek" television series.

SCIENTIFIC PRINCIPLES RELATED TO THE FILM

Energy

The fundamental physical principle depicted in the film is the concept of energy. We know that energy can take several different forms. It can appear as the motion of matter, as heat, as light, as an electrical current, as a chemical reaction, as nuclear or thermonuclear energy. The thermonuclear process powers our sun as well as all the stars. In its simplest form, this process can be viewed as bringing together four hydrogen nuclei (i.e., protons) to form a helium nucleus and release energy. The energy is due to the fact that the mass of the helium nucleus is less than the combined masses of the four hydrogen nuclei. The difference in mass has been converted into pure energy. Einstein had predicted the relationship between mass and energy in his famous formula $E=mc^2$, where E is the energy in joules, m is the mass in kilograms, and c is the speed of light, which equals 3×10^8 meters/second. Thus, mass itself is simply another form of energy.

The most general law of physics relates to energy. It can be stated simply:

Energy cannot be created or destroyed. It may be transformed
from one form into another, but the total amount of energy
never changes.

There are various kinds of energy that have been given specific names. Work is one such form of energy. The work, W, done on an object by an applied force, F, that moves the object a distance, d, is given by $W=Fd$, providing the force acts in the direction the object moves. Thus if we lift a weight twice as high, we do twice as much work because the distance moved is twice as great. Similarly, if we lift twice as heavy a weight through the same distance we do twice as much work because the force required is twice as great. Note that by this definition no work is required if you stand motionless holding a heavy weight, since the weight has not moved.

When work is applied to an object it can be converted into kinetic energy, potential energy, or heat (often due to friction). Kinetic energy is the energy of motion. If m is the mass of an object and v is its velocity, the kinetic energy, KE, is given by $KE=mv^2/2$. As an example, suppose a car of mass 1,000 kilograms were moving at a velocity of 26.8 meters per second (60 miles per hour) and it was slowed down by a force, F, of 5,000 newtons (kilogram meters/seconds^2). Since the work required to stop a car equals its kinetic energy, the distance, d, required for it to come to a complete stop would be $d=mv^2/(2F)=1,000$ kilograms $\times(26.8$ meters/ sec$)^2/(2\times5,000$ newtons$)=71.8$ meters. This is a realistic example of the stopping distance on a dry road after the brakes are applied. Note that the stopping distance increases as the square of the velocity. The kinetic energy of the car is converted into heat due to friction between the tires of the car and the road surface.

Potential energy is energy stored in an object by virtue of its position or shape. Thus a compressed spring has a potential energy. The potential energy of an object raised above the ground is called gravitational potential energy and equals the work done against gravity in raising the object. Potential energy is so named because it has the potential for doing work.

Power is defined as work done or energy expended divided by the time period it takes to do the work or to expend the energy. The unit of energy in the metric system is the *joule*, which equals one newton-meter. The unit of power in the metric system is the *watt*, which equals one joule per second (one kilowatt $=1,000$ watts).

SCIENTIFIC COMMENTARY

Relativity.   The opening of the film describes a spaceship traveling at greater than the speed of light. This is at present considered physically impossible. Light itself is the only entity that can travel at the speed of light. Any object with a non-zero rest mass cannot travel at the speed of light, since its mass would become infinite according to Einstein's theory of relativity. The crew members appear to be somehow buffered by devices emitting green light beams as they pass from faster-than-light speed to slower-than-light speed. No mechanism is alluded to, nor can a plausible one be conceived of, since travel at speeds faster than light is impossible.

Navigation.   As the spaceship approaches the planet, the commander orders the crew to change the "float." The angle of the model inside the plastic sphere on the navigational table then changes its direction. Presumably all of this represents a change in the orientation of the ship as it comes in to land.

Astronomy.   The ship "arranges its own eclipse" of the sun. It is not clear whether this means the ship passed behind a planet that obscured the sun Altair or whether it merely covered the image of Altair striking the viewscreen.

Gravity. The commander informs his crew that the gravity on the planet is only .897 of Earth gravity. He then instructs the crew members to adjust their equipment accordingly. This suggests that each crew member can alter gravity in some way. We know of no mechanism for doing this; however, artificial "gravity" can be created by rotating an object. For example, someone standing on the edge of a rapidly turning merry-go-round will feel a "pull" toward the rim of the merry-go-round. An individual whose eyes are shut might mistake the sensation for the pull of gravity. But it is not, of course, real gravity. Furthermore, this principle could not be used to create artificial gravity around a stationary astronaut who is standing on an alien planet, since no rotation would be taking place. Someone weighing 100 lbs. on Earth would weigh only 89.7 lbs. on Altair IV.

• Other statements concerning the operation of the spacecraft are also difficult to decipher. "Standby to reverse polarity" is a meaningless phrase in the absence of further information about the spaceship. The order to turn off the artificial gravity inside the spaceship could only be achieved by stopping the rotation of the circular shaped spaceship.

Atmosphere. The statement that the oxygen level is 4 is meaningless without stating the units of measurement. If it were 4 times that on Earth, the level would be toxic.

Energy. Robby the robot apparently is able to simulate the operation of the giant Krell machine on a more modest scale by converting energy into molecules of whatever substance is desired. Clearly, the robot would need an immense energy source to be able to create many tons of lead shielding, for example. Perhaps it plugs itself into the Krell thermonuclear power generators in some way when creating matter.

Telepathy. It is not clear why the tiger is so tame in the first sequence, in which it approaches Altaira. It would seem as if the tiger was able to interact telepathically with Altaira. Later, after she falls in love with Commander Adams, the tiger attacks her. Once again, what could it have sensed that was different at an observable level? Only if the beast was able to interact with her subconscious might it have found her to be changed. Since some animals are sensitive to changes in the emotional states of humans (i.e., can sense whether they are afraid or angry), perhaps the tiger could sense that Altaira was in love and therefore had lost her childlike innocence.

Biology.   Supposedly the Krell visited Earth over 200,000 years ago. Yet, the animal specimens that they brought back to Altair IV did not exist on Earth in the forms depicted in the film until much more recent times. It is very unlikely that animals transported to an alien planet would have evolved exactly the same way as the species did on Earth.

Relativity.   In attempting to contact Earth for instructions, one of the crew states that they have to short-circuit the continuum on a five or six parsec level. Since a parsec equals the distance that light travels in 3.26 years (i.e., equals 3.26 light years, or 19.2 trillion miles), this distance is huge and would result in a very long "short circuit"; moreover, it would seem to be impossible to short-circuit the space continuum.

Nuclear Physics.   Robby claims that the lead he is supplying to the expedition is much lighter than ordinary lead. Yet he calls it isotope 217. Isotopes of lead differ in the number of neutrons in the nucleus, while all have 82 protons. Lead 217 would have 217 neutrons and protons and actually be 5% heavier than lead 207, the common isotope.

Matter.   When Dr. Morbius describes the properties of Krell metal, he says that the molecules are many times *more dense* than earthly steel but are not made of *different* molecules. It is hard to see how one can substantially change the packing factor of similar molecules in a material. Morbius also says that the Krell metal drinks up energy like a sponge and is not made warm by the Commander's blaster. This property is also difficult to understand.

Neurology.   Dr. Morbius was able to build Robby only after his IQ was permanently increased by the Krell teaching machine. The ship's doctor has an IQ of 160 but it registers on the teaching machine as only one-third of Morbius's IQ. The process by which the teaching machine permanently altered Morbius's IQ is not easy to explain. Did it give him conscious access to a portion of the human mind that the rest of us are unable to utilize, and/or did it transmit additional knowledge from the Krell learning machine directly into his brain? Later, Dr. Ostrow appears to have knowledge of the Krell immediately after taking a "brain boost"; this occurrence suggests the theory of direct transmission of knowledge from the machine.

Scientific Notation.   Morbius, in describing the Krell power plants, says that they can produce the energy recorded on the dials in the laboratory, which can measure energy units totaling "10 raised almost literally to the power infinity." That statement is nonsense. There were perhaps 30 or 40 dials, which would represent an energy output of 10^{30} to 10^{40} energy units, which is most certainly not infinity.

Engineering. The size of the Krell machine and power plants is said by Dr. Morbius to be a cube 20 miles on each side, hence a volume of $20 \times 20 \times 20 = 8,000$ cubic miles. Later, Morbius states that this great machine is powered by 9,200 thermonuclear reactors buried 50 miles beneath the planet's surface. Is the 50-mile dimension inconsistent with the 20-mile dimension stated above for the Krell machine, or does it mean that the power plants were all located below the 8,000-cubic-mile-large machine?

Radiation. Morbius cautions his visitors not to look directly into the thermonuclear furnace but rather to view it indirectly with a mirror. He says that "man may not look on the Gorgon's face and live"—a reference to the Medusa legend. If looking directly into the furnace was fatal, presumably because of radiation, then turning one's back on the radiation to view the mirror's image would be equally deadly.

Energy. It is probable that the great Krell machine could only be activated by the subconscious thoughts of a powerful mind. Morbius has such a mind after exposure to the Krell educational machine. The other members of his expedition, as well as those of the rescue expedition, did not have minds powerful enough to trigger the Krell machine; as Morbius says to Adams, "You don't need brains to be a commander." Ordinary humans have detectable brain waves, and Morbius's stronger brain waves can activate the great Krell machine.

Biology. The footprint of the creature is a "biological nightmare." It walks as a biped yet has a paw print like a quadruped and a claw like a tree sloth, a combination indicative of its being the chimeric mental creation of an irrational subconscious.

Psychology. Morbius subconsciously knows that the rescue expedition is in danger from the creature. Consciously, he does not know he is responsible.
• When the creature again attacks the rescue expedition, why is it created outside their defense circle rather than within it? Perhaps it is Morbius's subconscious desire to terrorize the rescuers before attacking them.

Energy and Telepathy. As the creature attacks the rescue expedition, the film shows that a number of the energy dials in the Krell laboratory are lighted indicating the high energy output going into creating the monster. Altaira is awakened by a nightmare of the attack. Apparently her mind is sensitive to the monster created by the great Krell machine — perhaps she can sense the workings of her father's mind or can sense danger to Commander Adams.

Nuclear Physics. The monster cannot be destroyed by the weapons of Adams and his crew because its molecular structure is being renewed every microsecond. The statement that the neutron beams are 3 billion volts must refer to the internal workings of the machine generating the beams, since neutrons themselves are uncharged electrically and could not be directly affected by any electrical potential, no matter how great.

Robotics. When Morbius orders Robby to kill the monster, its built-in injunction against killing any intelligent being paralyzes the robot because it knows that the monster originated in Dr. Morbius's own subconscious and that in order to kill the monster it must kill Dr. Morbius. Apparently Robby is only temporarily deactivated, since we see the robot fully functional at the end of the film, despite Dr. Morbius's earlier statement that Robby's circuits would burn out if ordered to kill someone and the order was not promptly countermanded.

Energy. The dials indicating the energy drawn from the Krell furnaces light up graphically as the monster attempts to break into the laboratory. Presumably some of this energy is being used to melt the door. This is a very visual illustration of power consumption. Similarly, as Dr. Morbius collapses the rows of dials go dark, indicating that the power consumption is dropping back to zero.

Energy and Mass. The explosion of the entire planet is implausible. Even the most powerful 9,200 thermonuclear explosions detonated on Earth should not destroy an entire planet. Since the gravity on the surface of the planet is nearly equal to that on Earth, if it has a similar density, then the size of the planet would be similar to that of Earth. Not even the simultaneous explosions of 9,200 of our most powerful hydrogen bombs would destroy the Earth. One can only infer that the thermonuclear power plants on the Krell planet will each produce an immensely greater explosion than any hydrogen bomb built on Earth.

Is it likely that the Krell would build a simple mechanism to destroy their entire planet? Could the device have been installed by Morbius to insure that the Krell technology did not fall into the wrong hands?

Also, why does the departing rescue expedition take 24 hours to travel 100 million miles away from the planet when they can travel faster than light? It takes light less than 10 minutes to travel this distance.

CLASSROOM ACTIVITIES

Exercises to Extend Learning

1. At the beginning of the film, how fast is the spaceship traveling?

2. The spaceship is said to "arrange its own eclipse" of the sun. What does this mean?

3. The commander tells the crew that the gravity on Altair IV is .897 that of Earth's gravity. How much would someone who weighs 100 lbs. on Earth weigh on Altair IV?

4. The oxygen level on Altair IV is said to be 4. If this were four times the oxygen level on the surface of the Earth, could humans survive in it?

5. The film depicts several animals from Earth. Since the Krells' last visit to Earth was over 200,000 years ago, what did the ancestors of the deer and tiger look like? Is it likely that these animals would have evolved on an alien planet exactly as they evolved on Earth?

6. When Robby the Robot delivers lead shielding to the rescue expedition, it is stated that this lead is lighter than ordinary lead. Is the film correct about this? What isotope of lead was delivered? What is the isotope number of ordinary lead? What does the word *isotope* mean?

7. When Morbius describes the properties of Krell metal, he says that the molecules are more dense than those of earthly steel but are not made up of different molecules. What does he mean by "dense"?

8. What do you think the "brain boost" does to the individual receiving it?

9. Approximately how many dials do you see on the wall of the Krell laboratory? What is the total power output of the last dial in terms of the units on the first dial? Is the "10 raised almost literally to the power infinity" stated in the film correct for the total power output depicted in the Krell laboratory?

10. How big is the great Krell machine described by Morbius? How far below the surface are the thermonuclear reactors that power the Krell machine? Are the thermonuclear reactors inside or outside of the great Krell machine?

11. Morbius cautions his visitors not to look directly into the thermonuclear furnace. How, then, do they view it? Is this, in fact, a safe way to look inside a thermonuclear furnace? If not, why not?

12. When the monster attacks the rescue expedition, is it created inside the ship's defensive screen or outside of it?

13. When the monster attacks the rescue expedition, the film shows a number of energy dials lighting up in the Krell laboratory. Where is the energy going?

14. Why are the weapons of the rescue expedition ineffective against the monster?

15. At the end of the film, how long does it take the rescue expedition to travel 100 million miles away from Altair IV? How long would it take light to travel that distance?

16. Where does Robby the Robot get the energy to convert into matter and also to power himself?

Topics for Further Discussion

Robotics.   What was the power source for Robby? It could not have been completely self-contained because the robot could not possibly have enough energy to convert into many tons of lead, for example. On the other hand, the robot could not have drawn all of its power from the Krell furnaces, since it was not deactivated when it left the planet. Probably it had an internal power source and, in addition, was able to draw energy from the Krell furnaces.

• The rules of conduct programmed into Robby are virtually identical with those suggested by Isaac Asimov for robots, namely: (1) a robot may not injure a human being or through its inaction allow a human being to be injured; (2) a robot must obey an order given it by a human being except when obeying it would conflict with law number one; (3) a robot must protect its own existence except when such action would violate laws number one and number two. Should these rules be programmed into all robots?

• Compare the capabilities and behavior of Robby with other famous film robots or computers. The robots might include the giant alien robot Gort from *The Day the Earth Stood Still*; the robots in *Futureworld* and *Westworld*; the robots in *Bladerunner*; Huey and Dewey in *Silent Running*; and, of course, R2D2 and C3PO from the *Star Wars* trilogy; the computers could include Colossus from the movie of the same name; HAL from *2001* and *2010*; and the computer from *War Games*.

Anthropology. Why did Dr. Morbius not know more about the physical appearance of the Krell? At one point he plays a recording of Krell music: Is it not reasonable to suggest that there would have been visual recordings of the Krell as well? Would the Krell not have used computers, which could have transmitted information about their appearance? Furthermore, why were there no remains of the Krell or their structures? On Earth, skeletons millions of years old have been discovered. The Krell vanished a mere 200,000 years ago. Surely some remains would have been found to aid in reconstructing their appearance.

Ethics. Does Morbius, as a researcher, have the right to withhold his findings? Should physicists have been able to restrict knowledge of atom-splitting that would permit the making of atomic bombs?

• Since Commander Adams knows that Dr. Morbius is the creator of the monster, he shows great restraint in not killing Morbius in order to save Altaira and himself. Adams does draw his blaster, and one can only speculate as to his course of action if the monster had actually entered the laboratory. Would Adams have knocked out Morbius in an attempt to, at least temporarily, knock out his subconscious, or would Adams have been forced to kill Morbius?

Psychology. Psychologists have described elements of the Electra complex and incestuous feelings as factors in the relationships between fathers and daughters. Are such feelings hinted at in this film? What problems might a father and daughter marooned alone face, perhaps subconsciously, since they are also a man and a woman? What solutions might be devised?

Literature. What literary significance do you find in the following (answers are given in parentheses after each question):

(a) the young man who wins Altaira is named Adams (*referring to Adam and Eve*)

(b) the first spaceship to Altair IV was named the *Bellerophon* (*like the Greek hero, it was destroyed for angering the "gods," in this case Morbius and the great Krell machine*)

(c) the power plants are likened to the Gorgon's face (*looking at the Gorgon's face would turn the viewer into stone*)

(d) the man who came to care more for the Krell and Altair IV than for humans and Earth is named Morbius (*named after the god of dreams*)

(e) the line, "We are, after all, not God" (*the rescue expedition is unable to take the "godlike" Krell technology back to Earth*)

Government. Compare Morbius's statement that he alone is fit to determine which parts of the Krell knowledge are to be released to humanity with the government's decision to withhold information from the public in *The Day the Earth Caught Fire* (Chapter 2).

LITERARY COMMENTARY

William Shakespeare's play *The Tempest* provided the storyline for the film *Forbidden Planet*. In the play, Prospero and his daughter, Miranda, are living on an isolated island where Prospero can study and practice his magic. Ariel, an airy spirit, is Prospero's good servant. Already on the island when they arrived was Caliban, the son of a witch and a devil, deformed in appearance and lustful, jealous, greedy, and destructive in action. For the film, the island becomes the planet Altair IV; Prospero the magician becomes Morbius the scientist; magic becomes Krell science; Miranda becomes Altaira; Robby the Robot takes the place of Ariel; and Caliban is transformed into the "monster of the id."

In the play a storm casts a ship onto the island and introduces more characters, among them Ferdinand, who falls in love with Miranda. The ship also carries Stephano and Trinculo, low characters who lust after Miranda, plot to kill Prospero, and lose themselves in drunken revelry. In the film Captain Adams, as the Ferdinand character, falls in love with Altaira. Farman and the cook act the roles of Stephano and Trinculo: Farman attempts to seduce Altaira, and the cook gets drunk; both of them lie easily. The "monster of the id" controls them both.

At the conclusion of the play, Prospero renounces his magic, frees Ariel, acknowledges his responsibility for Caliban, and returns to the mainland with those from the ship. His "ending is despair," however, unless God's judgment reprieves him. Ferdinand and Miranda will be married, and their ending is thus a happy one. The film concludes more darkly because Morbius refuses to abandon the Krell science or to acknowledge the "monster of the id" until it is too late to save himself. He and his "magic" thus die together, although the happy ending survives in the C57D's escape to Earth, with the freed Robby serving as ship's navigator and with Altaira and Adams, who will be married.

Some of the film's peculiarities probably derive from the mingling of a seventeenth-century play, Freudian psychology, and a futuristic interpretation of both. Magic can be either good (white magic) or bad (black magic), the two kinds distinguishable only by their respective sources (angels and demons) and their effects (beneficial or harmful). All magic is suspect because of the near-impossibility of telling white magic from black. The magician's spiritual purity is the ultimate determiner. Morbius has idealized the Krell, elevating them almost to deities. His motives seem to him good: protecting his daughter's innocence, saving the men of the C57D from the demonic force that killed his own shipmates earlier, and preserving his ability to learn even more from the Krell science.

These motives are not pure, however. By preserving his daughter's innocence, he also restricts her life unnaturally. He selfishly retains her companionship and an unnatural degree of control over her affections and activities. While saving the men of the C57D, he also refuses them access to the Krell science and thus retains his mental superiority. By preserving his ability to learn more from the Krell science, he isolates himself still further from normal human beings and becomes less human himself.

Altaira, too, exhibits an "impure" character. Symbolically, her innocence and purity are established both by the kissing scene with Farman, which she sees as a dispassionate experiment to stimulate health, and by the scene with her "friends," the deer and the tiger. Just as only a pure and chaste woman could "tame" a unicorn, a pure and chaste woman could exercise some control over any wild beast, mythologically speaking. Thus the tiger is her "friend" while she remains pure, but once she has been "corrupted" by her love for Adams, the tiger turns on her. Her innocence in the kissing scene and the nude bathing scene is also countered by three other scenes. After Adams has told her to wear more concealing clothing, she coyly instructs Robby to make her something that covers her but that "fits in all the right places," that is, in fact, seductive. When she appears at the ship site to watch the men setting up their defenses, she says that her father has ordered her to stay away from the ship, "but this is far enough." She is disobeying her father in spirit, and she knows it. Finally, she shares her father's dreams of the monster's attack on the ship and wakes him, thus ending the attack. Her inner conflict between her love for her father and her love for Adams surfaces in this scene. The shared dream symbolizes some complicity with her father; the interruption of that dream symbolizes the shift of her loyalties from father to lover. The transference of love and loyalty becomes explicit when she countermands Robby's order to admit no one to the house and lets Adams and Ostrow into the house and her father's study during the night.

Freud theorized three parts to the personality: the superego, the ego, and the id. The superego is like a conscience, controlling and suppressing a person's nastier desires, fears, and actions. Those suppressed desires, fears, and actions, then, are not consciously recognized, and they form the id, the "monster" within each of us. According to Freudian theory, the id often surfaces in dreams and the content of dreams represents the dark side of a person. The conscious part of the mind, the public person known to himself and others, forms the ego. This Freudian concept, initially an attempt to characterize the personality of an individual, can also be applied to a group. Thus, among the group on Altair IV, the superego consists of Robby, with his injunction against harm to humans, and Altaira, who interrupts her father's destructive dream, opens the house to Adams and Ostrow, and helps them destroy the "monster of the id." The ego, the conscious part of the mind, consists of Adams and Ostrow, normal intelligent people who follow orders and otherwise act only for self-preservation or for the protection of those for whom they are responsible. The id, that dark underside of the mind, surfaces in Farman and the cook, but it is most apparent in Morbius, for the "monster of the id" is his creation. Its raging destruction represents his subconscious desires to retain possession of his daughter, to kill those who intrude into his private preserve, and to pursue his Faustian search for godlike knowledge and power. The film implies that he also destroyed the members of the earlier crew so that he could retain the Krell knowledge and power for himself.

CHAPTER BIBLIOGRAPHY

Film References

Clarke, Frederick S., and Steve Rubin. "Making *Forbidden Planet.*" *Cinefantastique* 8 (Spring 1979): 4–67.

Morsberger, Robert E. "Shakespeare and Science Fiction." *Shakespeare Quarterly* 12 (Spring 1961): 161.

Rubin, Steve. "Retrospect: *Forbidden Planet.*" *Cinefantastique* 4 (1975): 5–13.

Sutton, Martin. "Superego Confrontation on *Forbidden Planet.*" *Omni's Screen Flights/Screen Fantasies*. Ed. Danny Peary. Garden City, NY: Dolphin-Doubleday, 1984, pp. 112–16.

Warren, Bill. "*Forbidden Planet.*" *Keep Watching the Skies! American Science Fiction Movies of the Fifties: Volume One, 1950–1957*. Jefferson, NC: McFarland, 1982, pp. 261–74.

Film Reviews

National Parent Teacher 50 (May 1956): 39.
New Yorker 32, 12 May 1956: 171.
Newsweek 47, 4 June 1956: 98.
Saturday Review 39, 7 April 1956: 23.
Scholastic 68, 26 April 1956: 29.
Time 67, 9 April 1956: 112 ff.

Novelization

Stuart, W. J. *Forbidden Planet*. New York: Farrar, Straus & Cudahy, 1956.

CHAPTER 2

The Day the Earth Caught Fire

- British Lion/Pax (Great Britain), 1962, black and white, 99 minutes
- **Credits:** *Producer/director*, Val Guest; *screenplay*, Wolf Mankowitz and Val Guest; *cinematographer*, Harry Waxman; *special effects*, Les Bowie; *technical advisor*, Arthur Christiansen; *music*, Monty Norman
- **Cast:** Edward Judd (Peter Stenning), Janet Munro (Jeannie Craig), and Leo McKern (Bill McGuire)
- **Distributors:** *16 mm*—Ivy Film, 165 West 46th St., Room 414, New York, NY 10036, (212) 382-0111; *Videotape*—Thorn EMI Video, 1370 Ave. of the Americas, New York, NY 10019

PLOT SUMMARY

The movie opens in the offices of a major British newspaper. Peculiar changes in weather are being reported from around the world. These have followed the simultaneous explosions by the Russians (in Siberia) and the Americans (in Antarctica) of the two largest hydrogen bombs ever built. The leading character, Peter Stenning, is a reporter for the newspaper. He has been drinking heavily in the wake of a divorce that has resulted in his being prevented from seeing his son except in the presence of the boy's nanny. The reporter meets a government employee, Jeannie Craig, who leaks to him the information that the Earth's axis of rotation has been changed by the explosions. This has resulted in the dramatic weather changes reported around the globe, an eclipse of the Sun that occurs 10 days earlier than expected, and an unusual heat mist that rises four stories above ground level. The newspapermen conclude that this heat mist is due to changes in the flow of undersea currents caused in turn by the change in rotation of the Earth.

The woman is fired and briefly imprisoned for passing on this information, which government officials finally confirm. She then comes to work for the paper, and we find that humanity's troubles are only beginning: the newspaper learns from its Moscow correspondent that the ex-

16

plosions have done more than change the axis of the Earth's rotation. The planet is moving toward the Sun.

Temperatures continue to rise dramatically, and finally water is shut off to all dwellings. Water must be obtained at government-run facilities, which also have public baths. The elevated temperature has evaporated most of the drinkable water in Great Britain. While some of London's population seek relief in the country and others carry on their duties with grim dedication, part of the city's population riots. The reporter rescues his girlfriend from some of the rioters and barricades her apartment until the worst is over.

The government announces that four additional giant bombs will be exploded in Siberia to try to halt the motion of the Earth toward the Sun. At the end of the film we do not know whether these explosions have been successful. We see two preset headlines at the newspaper, "World Saved" and "World Doomed."

Special Effects.   The special effects are minimal, with the eclipse, fog scenes, and cyclones being the main examples. The film also utilizes stock catastrophe footage and has graphic scenes of overheated residents seeking water at a government installation or departing for the country.

Much of the movie was filmed inside an actual British newspaper, and some of the cast were real newspaper employees. The newsroom and production room scenes are therefore quite realistic.

SCIENTIFIC PRINCIPLES RELATED TO THE FILM

Momentum

The fundamental physical principle depicted in the film is the concept of conservation of momentum. Linear momentum is defined as the product of the mass, m, of an object and its velocity, v (i.e., linear momentum $= mv$). Linear momentum is a vector quantity, having a magnitude and a direction.

When the resultant external force on an object or group of objects is zero, from Newton's second law (Resultant Force $=$ mass $\times$ acceleration), the acceleration of the object is also zero. But a zero acceleration means that the velocity remains constant in time. Therefore, the linear momentum remains constant in time. This can be summarized as follows:

Linear momentum is constant in time in a system on which there are no *net* external forces.

For example, if two equally strong men push in opposite directions on a car, the pushes are canceled, the net force is zero, and the linear momentum of the car remains constant in time.

This concept is particularly important in understanding what happens during the firing of a rocket or gun. Let M be the mass of a rifle and m be the mass of a bullet that it fires, and let v and V be the respective velocities of each (see Figure 2.1a). Before the bullet is fired, the momentum of the rifle plus bullet is zero, since both have zero velocity. After the bullet is fired, the linear momentum of the rifle and the bullet, which move in opposite directions (Figure 2.1b), remains zero. Thus $0 = Mv - mV$.

Exactly the same principle is involved in all rockets. In that case, hot gases of mass, m, are exhausted at high speed out of the rear of the rocket. The linear momentum, mV, of these hot gases being emitted backwards causes the main body, M, of the rocket to move forward with the velocity, v, such that $0 = Mv - mV$ once again.

Mass of the Earth/Nuclear Explosion

In *The Day the Earth Caught Fire*, the explosion of two simultaneous hydrogen bombs supposedly pushes the Earth toward the Sun, as depicted in Figure 2.2. Let us consider the physics involved. The mass of the Earth is 6×10^{24} kilograms, which is equivalent to 6.6×10^{21} tons. The largest hydrogen bomb exploded to date released energy equivalent to an explosion of 68 million tons of TNT, which we round upward to 100 million (i.e., 10^8) tons of TNT. (Note that tons of TNT are thus units of energy.) For the Earth to be moved toward the Sun, some of the matter would have to be propelled in the direction away from the Sun at sufficient speed to escape the Earth's gravitational pull, that is, at speeds greater than the escape velocity of 25,000 miles per hour. Let us assume that the atomic explosion was sufficient to hurl 10^8 tons of debris at the escape velocity of 25,000 miles per hour. Then, from the conservation of linear momentum of the Earth: $0 = (10^8 \text{ tons} \times 25,000 \text{ mph}) - (6 \times 10^{21} \text{ tons} \times V \text{mph})$; solving for V, we get $V = 4.2 \times 10^{-10}$ mph. Multiplying this by 8.8×10^3 hours per year reveals that in one year the Earth would have moved only about 3.7×10^{-6} miles (or about $1/4$ inch) closer to the Sun! Since the average distance of Earth from the Sun is 93×10^6 miles, this motion would not have been noticeable. It should also be noted that it would take hydrogen bombs of much greater explosive power than 10^8 tons of TNT to hurl 10^8 tons of debris at speeds equal to the escape velocity. As the explosive power of the hydrogen bomb is increased, there is a possibility that the detonation itself may cause worldwide destruc-

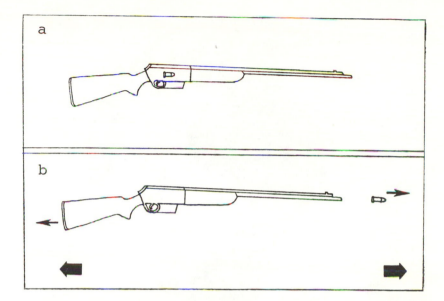

FIGURE 2.1. The conservation of momentum principle applied to the firing of a rifle: (*a*) Both the rifle and bullet are at rest; (*b*) The bullet is fired to the right while the rifle recoils to the left. The two equal heavy arrows represent the equal momenta of the rifle and bullet.

tion. However, any explosion too small to destroy all life on Earth immediately by its blast would also be too small to move the Earth appreciably toward the Sun.

In our calculation of the possible effect on the Earth of hurling 10^8 tons of debris at the escape velocity, we have neglected the fact that the Earth turns on its axis once every 24 hours and, in addition, is moving in a nearly circular orbit around the Sun. Including these rotational effects (and the related conservation of angular momentum) in the analysis of what would happen to the Earth if 10^8 tons of debris were blasted into outer space is extremely complicated. We can be certain, however, that the net change in the result would be too small to change our conclusion that the motion of the Earth toward the Sun would not be appreciable. In addition, matter hurled from the Earth at the escape velocity would continually slow down as the mass traveled farther from Earth, and as this happened, the Earth's velocity toward the Sun would also slow to zero. At the initial moment of explosion, however, the results obtained from the calculation we performed would be approximately correct. The

FIGURE 2.2. The two arrows represent the momentum of the debris hurled from the Earth by a thermonuclear explosion and the momentum (identical in magnitude) of the Earth as it recoils in the opposite direction.

important point is that the actual motion of the Earth toward the Sun would be even less than the $1/4$ inch per year, calculated above.

Another way to look at the unlikelihood of an atomic explosion's throwing the Earth out of orbit is to consider the greatest explosion of the past century. That was the volcanic explosion on the island of Krakatoa in 1883. One estimate of the force of that explosion (*Guiness Book of World Records*, 1980, p. 134) was that it was equivalent to 26 times the power of the greatest hydrogen bomb detonation, that is $26 \times 68,000,000 = 1,768,000,000$ tons of TNT. Rocks were thrown to a height of 34 miles, and dust fell 10 days later at a distance of over 3,000 miles. The explosion was recorded 2,968 miles away, four hours after it occurred, as "the roar of heavy guns." In fact, the explosion was heard over $1/13$ the surface of the entire Earth.

Probably the greatest explosion in recorded history blew the island of Thera, near Crete, to pieces in approximately 1500 B.C. Guiness estimates that volcanic explosion to have been five times larger than the Krakatoa blast, that is, equivalent to $5 \times 1,768,000,000 = 8,840,000,000$ tons of TNT. The Thera explosion and the tidal waves caused by it may have been the basis for the Atlantis legend referred to by Plato, but it did not change the axis of rotation of the Earth or alter the orbit of the Earth around the Sun. Remember that the Thera explosion is estimated to have been about 130 times greater than the largest hydrogen bomb exploded.

SCIENTIFIC COMMENTARY

Atmospheric Science. The interference in radio and television reception could have been due to disruption in the ionosphere caused by the explosions. That would affect the bouncing of radio and television waves off this layer of our atmosphere.

Astronomy. The premature solar eclipse was clear evidence that something had happened to either the orbit of the Earth or its rotation about its axis or both. A solar eclipse is caused by the relative position of the Sun, the Earth, and the Moon. One can calculate solar eclipses for any position on the surface of the Earth thousands of years in advance. It is therefore impossible to have an eclipse occur 10 days early unless something has happened to the orbit of one or more of these three bodies.

Weather. The heat mist was supposedly caused by cold water from the melting ice caps reaching warmer water, lowering its temperature, and then presumably cooling the humid air above it. This could produce a heat mist, but a four-story mist covering one-third of the globe seems implausible. The causes of the cyclones (Americans call cyclones "hurricanes") that followed the heat mist are unclear.

Geology. It is stated in the film that the Earth has changed its axis of rotation a number of times in the past. The Earth's magnetic field may have changed polarity (the north magnetic pole becoming the south magnetic and vice versa) many times during the history of the planet. These changes are inferred from studying the magnetism of particles that froze into rock forms at different times in the Earth's history. Iron particles in molten lava beds aligned themselves according to the magnetic field at the Earth's surface at the time these rocks solidified. The rocks then recorded the orientation of the magnetic field for an indefinitely long period of time. Such rocks have led some scientists to conclude that magnetic reversals have occurred over intervals of time as short as 35,000 years, although the cause for these reversals is unknown. Other scientists have suggested, however, that the apparent changes in the magnetic poles of the Earth were caused by continental drift (i.e., the drifting continents have moved the lava), and thus it is the rocks, not the magnetic poles, that have changed their orientation.

There is no evidence that the physical rotation of the Earth about its axis has changed to any appreciable degree in the past.

Physiology. An interesting question is the temperature at which society would cease to function. The newspaper indicates temperatures of 140° have been reached and are rising each day; at such temperatures most people would have collapsed from heat stroke, not continued to function to a limited degree, as pictured.

CLASSROOM ACTIVITIES

Exercises to Extend Learning

1. Was the eclipse of the Sun that occurs in the film an expected event? What causes an eclipse of the Sun? Can an eclipse of the Sun be calculated far in advance? What does it mean if an eclipse occurs at a time different from the calculated time?

2. How does the film explain the occurrence of the heat mist?

3. The film shows a cyclone. What do Americans call a cyclone? What produces a cyclone?

4. The film states that the Earth has changed its axis of rotation in the past. This is an incorrect statement. How could scientists infer that such a change had occurred?

5. How hot does it get by the end of the picture?

6. At how high a temperature could society still function?

7. What would the long period of elevated temperatures have done to the food chain on which we depend?

8. Even if the world was saved by the counterexplosions, would there likely have been so much dirt thrown into the atmosphere that a "nuclear winter" would result?

Topics for Further Discussion

Political Science. The movie belongs to the run of antinuclear films that were turned out in large numbers during the 1950s and early 1960s. In this film the news media is portrayed as seeking out the details of the problem and disclosing the truth to the public. Obviously, the government had suppressed the information in order to avoid panic, which might interfere with the building of the four counterbombs needed to save humanity. Was the government's course of action the correct one? Do you share the concern over the use of nuclear devices expressed in the film?

Communication.   Why didn't nongovernment scientists reveal the nature of the problems to the public much earlier? Any scientist should have known that there was an enormous problem when an unanticipated eclipse occurred. Furthermore, the extraordinarily bizarre weather should have alerted scientists that humanity was in danger. Is it plausible that *only* a newspaper reporter with no scientific background was able to uncover the tilt in the Earth's axis?

Sociology.   Whom would you believe, investigative reporters or official government spokespersons?
• How realistic was the behavior of the British population when faced with the announcement that the Earth was moving toward the Sun? Compare this behavior to their behavior during the Blitz in World War II and the 1981 riots caused by unemployment.

Physiology.   How high an external temperature can the human body stand for a sustained period before it becomes incapacitated or death occurs?

Films.   Relate this antinuclear film to others of the same period, such as *On the Beach, Dr. Strangelove, Them, These Are the Damned, Panic in Year Zero*, and *The War Game*.

LITERARY COMMENTARY

The 1962 film *The Day the Earth Caught Fire* comes from an original screenplay without a literary source. However, despite its dramatic focus on the decline and rise of Peter Stenning, newspaper reporter, the dominant theme of the film is the careless abuse of nuclear power and the resultant effects on the Earth and its population.

While the hazards of nuclear power have been a theme of science fiction since 1910, and a common theme since the 1930s, the theme usually deals specifically with war. In 1914, for example, H. G. Wells imagined civilization destroyed by atomic bombs in his novel *The World Set Free*. The classic novel of nuclear holocaust is Walter Miller's *A Canticle for Leibowitz* (1960), which shows civilization destroyed by atomic war, then slowly rebuilding itself over centuries until it destroys itself again by a second atomic war. As in *The Day the Earth Caught Fire, A Canticle for Leibowitz* implies that national competition, face-saving, and political secrecy cause the disaster. Unlike the film, however, Miller's novel provides a Christian and Catholic context that draws an analogy to the religious wars of the Reformation period. A more recent and ambiguous version of the holocaust novel is Frederik Pohl's *Terror* (1986). Pohl imagines the United States setting a "doomsday bomb" in the side of an undersea volcano so that it can cause huge tidal waves, cyclonic winds, and the kind of nuclear winter that some scientists now believe caused the extinction of the dinosaurs and other lifeforms 65 million years ago when a huge asteroid impacted the Earth. In Pohl's novel, terrorists seize control of the bomb and nearly succeed in detonating it. Although they fail, the military nonetheless leave the bomb in place, even though others might succeed, because they believe it is politically necessary.

Other science fiction novels deal with atomic bombs used carelessly and with ill effects to cure such problems as a severe water shortage or an impending large earthquake; still others deal with accidents in bomb tests or at atomic power plants. For examples, read Marta Randall's *Islands* (1976), in which coastal areas — and the Hawaiian Islands — are drowned by an error of judgment; or read Lester del Rey's *Nerves* (1956), which shows an accident in a nuclear power plant threatening to become a major disaster. Many of these stories focus on human survivors after such a holocaust. Two such works that have been adapted to film are Roger Zelazny's *Damnation Alley* (1969) and Harlan Ellison's "A Boy and His Dog" (1969).

Very few stories, mostly early and implausible fantasy, show any change in the Earth's orbit, but Larry Niven's "Inconstant Moon" (1971) does examine the possibility that the Sun has become a nova, which would cause the same results on Earth as the planet's spiraling into the Sun. The use of atomic power to change celestial orbits, not of the Earth but of comets or asteroids, occurs in various works, however. The film *Meteor* (1979) conveys such action, as does Greg Benford's and William Rotsler's novel *Shiva Descending* (1980).

Many science fiction works have dealt with the "accidents" resulting from nuclear tests, primarily in the form of radiation-caused mutations. *Them* is an example on film, and nearly every nuclear holocaust story or novel includes some mention of radiation-induced mutation. The closest literary analogue to *The Day the Earth Caught Fire*, though, is Douglas Warner's *Death on a Warm Wind* (1968), in which continuing atomic tests cause earthquakes, floods, strange winds, and millions of deaths. In this novel, as in the film, the problem is created and then compounded by governmental secrecy.

CHAPTER BIBLIOGRAPHY

Film Reviews

America 1006, 24 Mar. 1962: 840.
Commonweal 76, 6 April 1962: 39.
New Republic 146, 9 April 1962: 26.
New Yorker 38, 24 Mar. 1962: 149.
Newsweek 59, 5 Mar. 1962: 84.
Redbook 118 (April 1962): 20.
Saturday Review 45, 10 Feb. 1962: 35.
Seventeen 21 (April 1962): 42.
Time 79, 6 April 1962: 96.

CHAPTER 3

Destination Moon

- George Pal Productions/Eagle Lion (USA), 1950, color, 91 minutes
- **Credits:** *Producer*, George Pal; *director*, Irving Pichel; *screenplay*, Robert Heinlein, Rip van Ronkel, and James O'Hanlon, based on *Rocket Ship Galileo*, by Robert Heinlein; *cinematographer*, Lionel Lindon; *astronomical arts*, Chelsey Bonnestell; *animation sequences*, Walter Lantz; *music*, Leith Stevens
- **Cast:** John Archer (James Barnes), Warner Anderson (Charles Cargraves), Tom Powers (General Thayer), and Dick Wesson (Joe Sweeney)
- **Distributors:** *16 mm* — Ivy Film, 165 West 46th Street, Room 414, New York, NY 10036, (212) 382-0111; *Videotape* — The Nostalgia Merchant, 6255 Sunset Blvd., Suite 1019, Hollywood, CA 90028

PLOT SUMMARY

As the film opens, a rocket is fired on a military testing range. Its builder is Charles Cargraves, a noted rocket expert. The firing is watched by General Thayer, who was forced out of the military because of his advocacy of rockets. The launching ends in disaster as the rocket falls back to Earth rather than going into orbit 12,000 miles above the Earth. Thayer tells Cargraves that this disaster will end government funding of rocket research.

Two years later, General Thayer visits the plant of a successful airplane manufacturer, James Barnes, and asks Barnes to support building a rocket to the Moon. Barnes then arranges a meeting of business tycoons at which the principles of space flight are explained through a Woody Woodpecker cartoon. The businessmen are told that the United States must get to the Moon first; Thayer warns them that whichever country can fire missiles from the Moon will control the Earth. Barnes asserts that the government will ultimately pay for the project if it is successful. The business leaders then decide to support the building of the Moon rocket.

As the rocket is completed, the government forbids the testing of its nuclear-powered engine because of public concern about possible radiation leakage. Barnes decides that they should launch the rocket, untested, before government officials block its firing. Thus, with only 19 hours to prepare for the launch, they decide to go ahead. The crew consists of Barnes, Cargraves, Thayer, and Joe Sweeney, who replaces the fourth crew member, sick with an appendicitis attack. The spaceship is named *Luna*.

The take-off is perfect. We see the effects of acceleration on the crew and, later, the effects of weightlessness. When the radar does not turn, due to the freezing of its lubricant by the extreme cold of outer space, members of the crew don spacesuits and go outside the ship to free the radar. Cargraves accidentally falls off the ship and is seen floating only yards away from it. Barnes rescues him using an oxygen cylinder as a propulsion system.

The landing on the Moon consumes more fuel than expected. The crew is congratulated by Washington on its achievement, and we see the landscape of the Moon. They then learn that they must substantially reduce the weight of the ship or they will not have enough fuel to return to Earth. Everything possible is thrown overboard. They are still 110 pounds too heavy and are about to draw lots to see who will remain behind when Sweeney settles the matter by going outside the ship in the only remaining spacesuit. Barnes then devises a way of bringing everyone home. First, he throws out the radio; then he has Sweeney remove the remaining spacesuit in the airlock and jettisons the suit after Sweeney has left the airlock. This reduces the weight of the ship by 120 pounds.

As they launch the spaceship successfully from the Moon, the movie ends. Our first trip to the Moon is a success, and the Moon has been claimed on behalf of the United States, in the service of all humanity.

Special Effects.   These are excellent, with extensive use of painted backgrounds and a clever matching of models, paintings, and rocketship interiors. This was also the first science fiction film made using 3-camera technicolor. The prior use of technicolor was for fantasy rather than science fiction.

SCIENTIFIC PRINCIPLES RELATED TO THE FILM

Gravity

Sir Isaac Newton was the first to realize that the same force that causes objects to fall to the Earth is also responsible for the orbit of the planets around the Sun and that of the Moon around the Earth. He stated that this force, gravity, acts according to the following equation: $F = Gm_1m_2 / r^2$, where F is the force, in newtons, between two spheres of mass, m_1 and m_2, in kilograms, whose centers are a distance, r, apart, in meters, as depicted in Figure 3.1. G is a constant of nature, the same everywhere in the universe, and has a value of 6.67×10^{-11} newton-meter^2 / kilogram^2. Using calculus, Newton later proved that one could treat each planet as a sphere, all of whose mass acted as though it was concentrated at the center, in calculating its effects on any objects located outside of the planet.

All mass attracts all other mass in the universe. The force of attraction falls off as the inverse of the square of the distance ($1/d^2$). Thus if you separate two masses by double their original distance, the gravitational force between them is reduced by a factor of 4.

It is the force of gravity that keeps the Moon, or any manmade satellite, in orbit around the Earth. It can be shown that any object that moves in a circle at constant speed is undergoing an acceleration because the *direction* of its speed changes continuously even though the magnitude of its speed is unchanged. In order for a satellite to move in a circle at constant speed there must be a net force acting on it. That force, the gravitational attraction of the Earth on the mass of the body moving around it, is commonly referred to as gravity. If the force of gravity on a satellite points to the center of the Earth, it is sometimes asked, why does the satellite not fall to the Earth? The answer is, why should it? Newton's second law states that the acceleration, a, is in the direction of the resultant force, F, on a body of mass, m. It does not state that the velocity itself is in the direction of the resultant force. In the case of the Moon's circular motion around the Earth, the rate of change of the Moon's

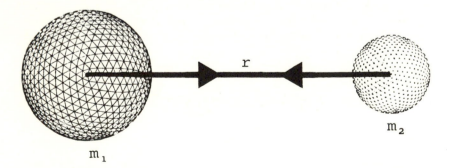

FIGURE 3.1.   The gravitational force of attraction between two spherically symmetric masses acts along the straight line, r, joining their centers.

velocity (i.e., its acceleration) can be shown to point to the center of the Earth.

For more complicated mass configurations, one would have to break the mass up into little spheres and then add all of the forces acting between these spheres in order to calculate the resultant force between two irregularly shaped masses.

It can be shown that any projectile fired from the surface of the Earth at a speed of less than 5 miles per second will fall to Earth. A projectile fired at an appropriate angle at speeds between 5 and 7 miles per second will go into orbit around the Earth. Any projectile fired at 7 miles per second or faster (the "escape velocity") will have enough initial kinetic energy permanently to leave the vicinity of the Earth. In other words, a spaceship must attain a velocity of at least 7 miles per second (or 25,000 miles per hour) to overcome the effects of the Earth's gravitational pull.

Next let us consider the gravitational force on an object of mass m on the surface of the Earth as shown in Figure 3.2. From Newton's law of gravity the force on the object $= Gm\ M/r^2$ where M, the mass of the

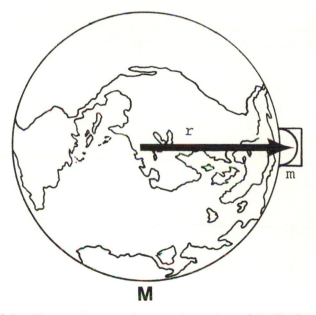

FIGURE 3.2.   The weight of an object on the surface of the Earth is the force of attraction between the mass of the Earth and the mass of the object.

Earth, is 6×10^{24} kilograms, and r, the radius of the Earth, is 6.4×10^6 meters. Substituting these figures into the above formula yields for the force on mass m, $F = m$ (6.67×10^{-11}) $(6 \times 10^{24})/(6.4 \times 10^6)$ $(6.4 \times 10^6) = m(9.8 \text{ meter/sec}^2)$. Thus the force of gravity on the surface of the Earth produces an acceleration due to gravity, g, of 9.8 meters/second² ($= 32$ feet/second²). The acceleration due to gravity on the surface of any planet depends upon both the mass and the radius of the planet. Table 3.1 presents similar calculations for the gravitational acceleration on the surface of several important members of our solar system.

The last column in the table gives the gravitational acceleration on the surface of the given body relative to that of the Earth. Thus, on the Moon, whose gravitational acceleration is only .16 that of the Earth, a 200-pound man (i.e., a man who weighed 200 pounds on Earth) would weigh $.16 \times 200 = 32$ pounds. The man's mass did not change, only the force of gravity acting on it.

On a planetary body whose gravitational acceleration is lower than that of the Earth, the escape velocity of a rocket is also lower. Therefore, it took less fuel for the astronauts who had landed on the Moon to take-off from the surface of the Moon and go into orbit about the Moon to rendezvous with the mother ship than this operation would have required from the surface of the Earth.

Astronauts in orbit around the Earth experience freefall, the apparent absence of gravity. This does not mean that there is no gravity acting on them, but rather that the entire force of gravity is being used to pull them into a circular orbit at constant speed around the Earth. None of the force of gravity is left over to pull them into the Earth. Another example of the illusion that gravity can be suspended could occur to a passenger in a closed elevator whose support cable snaps. The passenger would float in the elevator, and any object placed in the air would simply remain there. The passenger would be in freefall because the elevator cable has snapped, not because gravity has been suspended.

TABLE 3.1.   Gravitational Acceleration at the Surface of the Moon and Three Planets

Body	Mass (kg)	Average radius (m)	g at surface (m/s²)	g/g$_e$
Moon	7.4×10^{22}	1.7×10^6	1.6	.16
Venus	4.9×10^{24}	6.1×10^6	8.8	.89
Earth	6×10^{24}	6.4×10^6	9.8	1.00
Mars	6.4×10^{23}	3.4×10^6	3.7	.38

Momentum

Momentum is defined as the product of the mass, m, of an object and its velocity, v; that is, momentum $= mv$. Momentum is a vector quantity, having a magnitude and a direction.

When the resultant external force on an object or group of objects is zero, the acceleration of the object is also zero, since, from Newton's second law, it equals the resultant force divided by the mass. But a zero acceleration means that the velocity remains constant in time. Therefore the momentum remains constant in time. This can be summarized as follows:

Momentum is constant in time in a system on which there are no *net* external forces.

For example, if two equally strong men push in opposite directions on a car, the pushes are canceled, the net force is zero, and the momentum of the car remains constant in time.

This concept is particularly important in understanding what happens during the firing of a rocket or gun. Let M be the mass of a rifle and m be the mass of a bullet that it fires, and let v and V be their respective velocities. Before the bullet is fired, the momentum of the rifle plus bullet is zero, since both have zero velocity. After the bullet is fired, the momentum of the rifle and the bullet remains zero (refer to Figure 2.1). Thus, $0 = Mv - mV$.

Exactly the same principle is involved in all rockets. In that case hot gases of mass m are exhausted at high speed out of the rear of the rocket. The momentum, mV, of these hot gases being emitted backwards causes the main body of the rocket, M, to move forward with the velocity v such that $0 = Mv - mV$ once again.

SCIENTIFIC COMMENTARY

Rockets. The curved trail of the rocket in the sky as it malfunctioned seems out of proportion. The small curves suggest that the rocket was far away, but it crashed very close to the launching site.

Escape Velocity. General Thayer tells Barnes that the new nuclear-powered engine developed by Cargraves ejects the gases at 30,000 feet per second. This is only about 6 miles per second; it is less than the escape velocity of 7 miles per second necessary for the spaceship to pull free of

Earth's gravitational attraction. Thus, a greater mass of steam would have to be ejected out of the rear of the rocket at this speed than the entire remaining mass of the rocket in order to propel that remaining mass at escape velocity.

The nuclear engine that Cargraves was testing blew up after 1 hour and 23 minutes. Presumably the engine would not have to operate for that long a period throughout the round trip to the Moon.

Propulsion.   As a propellant the engine of the spaceship uses water heated to dry steam. Probably this means that the water is ejected as a gas of H_2O molecules.

Momentum.   The Woody Woodpecker short is a very accurate description of the conservation of momentum using as examples the firing of a rifle and the firing of a rocket. The distance to the Moon of 240,000 miles is correct, as is the statement that rockets will work in outer space (i.e., in a vacuum). The pull of gravity on the spaceship is depicted as being due to a magnet embedded in the Earth. The cartoon is excellent.

Metallurgy.   Barnes instructs someone over the telephone to use titanium because it is lighter. Titanium is lighter than steel but is heavier than aluminum; however, titanium's superior strength/weight ratio and ability to withstand higher temperatures make it a better choice than aluminum in such applications.

Rockets.   The decision to launch the spaceship on only 19 hours notice, with an untested engine, is unrealistic. The preparation and countdown for the Apollo missions took far longer than 19 hours.

• During the blast-off from Earth the rear of the spaceship appears to be emitting a flame. This is in contradiction to the use of water as the propellant to be exhausted as steam out of the rear of the vehicle.

Physiology.   The crew are all pressed against their couches during the take-off. The grimaces on their faces appear realistic, but none of them passes out as one might expect from the high acceleration characteristic of the distortions of their faces.

Gravity.   Cargraves correctly describes the apparent weightlessness inside the spaceship as being caused by everything falling together. For that reason he tells Sweeney that there is no danger of falling from the spaceship because everything inside it is in the same free orbit.

Biology. Our astronauts did complain of nausea when they were weightless. However, a human can swallow a pill while standing on his or her head; this suggests that gravity does not play a role in swallowing.

Spaceship. The size of the spaceship appears to be different at various times in the film. On Earth or on the Moon it appears to be 30 or 40 times taller than a man. In the outer-space sequence it appears to be only about 20 times taller.

Momentum and Weightless Environments. The use of the oxygen bottle as a small rocket is an excellent example of the conservation of momentum. The magnetic shoes for walking on the ship is a good idea, providing that the hull is made of a ferromagnetic material such as steel. The rope stays extended in the outer-space sequence, as it should in the absence of gravity.

Radar. A spokesman for the Dry Wells launching site stated that its staff would track the spaceship on radar as long as possible. There is a maximum distance over which a given radar installation can track a given object. This distance is determined by the power of the radar waves emitted, the size of the object from which the waves will be reflected, and the sensitivity of the detector for the reflected waves. Also, as the Earth turned on its axis, Dry Wells would eventually no longer be in a line-of-sight position with respect to the spaceship.

Moon. The surface of the Moon is reasonably accurately depicted, with one exception. The Moon actually has a fine powder on its surface rather than the irregularly shaped plates depicted in the film. This powdery surface is called the regolith and was caused by the bombardment of the surface of the Moon by small meteorites over billions of years.

The gravity on the surface of the Moon is $1/6$ that on the surface of the Earth, so that a 600-pound camera would weigh only 100 pounds on the Moon. This also accounts for the crew's ability to make incredible jumps on the surface of the Moon.

Communications. It does take a radio wave approximately 3 seconds to travel the 480,000 miles from the Earth to the Moon and back again.

Moon. The statement that it will remain midday on the Moon for a couple of days is correct. The Moon's day is approximately one month in length since it rotates on its axis only once per month.

Destination Moon: Charles Cargraves stands on the moon as James Barnes descends from the spaceship. The moon's surface is incorrectly depicted as being composed of flat platelets. (Photo: Museum of Modern Art/Film Stills Archive.)

Momentum.   "Reaction mass" refers to the mass of the water that is exhausted from the spaceship when the engine is turned on.

Rockets.   The landing of the spaceship on the Earth will use parachutes, in a manner similar to that employed by our Apollo spaceships.

CLASSROOM ACTIVITIES

Exercises to Extend Learning

1. General Thayer says that the new nuclear-powered engine developed by Cargraves ejects gas at 30,000 feet per second. Convert this speed to miles per second. How does this speed compare to the escape velocity of 7 miles per second from Earth?

2. According to the film, will a rocket ship work on the same principle in outer space as in the Earth's atmosphere?

3. During the lift-off of the spacecraft, does its rocket emit a
flame? In view of the propellant used, should the rocket have emitted a
flame?

4. Cargraves tells Sweeney that there is no danger of falling off the
spacecraft. Why did he say that?

5. Does the film show the astronauts to have trouble swallowing a
pill in the absence of gravity? Can a human swallow a pill standing upside
down? Does your answer to the second question contradict what the film
asserts about swallowing?

6. How big is the spaceship relative to the height of one of the
crewmen? Estimate your answer based on when the spaceship is on the
Earth, the Moon, and in outer space. Are all your estimates the same?

7. Dry Wells says that it will track the spaceship for as long as
possible. Why can't it track the spaceship all the way to the Moon?

8. How long does the film say it will remain midday on the Moon?
How long is one "day" on the Moon?

9. How long does the film say it will take a radio wave to travel
from the Earth to the Moon and return?

10. The surface of the Moon is accurately portrayed, with one exception. What is that exception?

Topics for Further Discussion

Political Science.   Do you think that it was proper to claim the
Moon in the name of the United States for the benefit of all of mankind?

Sociology.   Do you think that businessmen would actually risk vast
sums of money on a project that might fail?

Mass.   What would you leave behind if you had to lighten the spaceship?

LITERARY COMMENTARY

Both characters and plot in Heinlein's 1947 novel, *Rocket Ship Galileo*, betray its status as a "juvenile" novel, just as incidents in both film
and novel record Heinlein's well-known patriotism and Libertarian indi-
vidualism. The novel's major characters are three teenaged boys — Ross
Jenkins, Art Mueller, and Maurice Abrams — and Art's uncle, Dr. Donald

Cargraves. Although the boys squabble and tease like any teenagers, they also test model rockets in very scientific fashion. In a clearing on the Jenkins land, they have a test stand, dynamometer, and a reinforced concrete safety wall. They keep thorough records of their tests, including films as well as notes, thus demonstrating their knowledge of and belief in the scientific method. Ross's "hobbies" are chemistry and rocket fuels; Art's are radio and photography; Morrie's is astronomy. They work on their rockets in the high school shop, and they have completed a course in differential equations. Their high school, they tell Cargraves, is "progressive."

Cargraves, impressed by the boys' skill and knowledge, invites them to "go to the Moon" with him. He has tried to interest corporations in funding the project, but they have refused. Corporations have to show a profit, he says, and they see no profit in a trip to the Moon. A different situation exists in the film, of course.

But Cargraves has purchased a scrap "Atlantic freighter rocket" for a ship, and the boys compete for and win a $250,000 prize from a scientific competition for their funding. Cargraves can get fissionable material for experimental purposes, and the four of them will do all the work themselves under Cargraves's leadership. The boys become his apprentices as well as his workforce.

As in the film, the rocket construction takes place in the New Mexico desert and there is evidence of sabotage. A man with a temporary injunction against the rocket appears just minutes before take-off, but the rocket leaves anyway. On the flight out, Cargraves continues to instruct the boys, a theme also carried out in the film through the continuous lectures to Sweeney. The boys speculate that the Moon's craters are not volcanic or meteoritic but instead the result of "one atomic war too many" by the "Moon people." Unlike the film characters, they do not go outside the ship in space and they do not have a bad landing.

The novel's conclusion differs radically from the film's. In the film, the pilot uses too much reaction mass in his landing, and the drama and suspense arise from the need to lighten the ship sufficiently to lift-off. In the novel, after a fine landing, Morrie finds a piece of worked metal, sees someone, and has trouble with his air valve. The valve works fine later, and the man he has seen is dismissed as a hallucination from anoxia. Ultimately, though, Cargraves and the boys discover a Nazi base on the Moon. The man Morrie saw was one of them. The Nazis damage their ship, expecting them to die on the Moon. However, the boys' ingenuity triumphs. They capture the Nazi leader and his ship, learn his plans to control Earth with a missile base on the Moon, and discover that the Nazi base underground is in "the homes of the people of the Moon." Cargraves and the boys then return to Earth as international heroes. In the few years between the novel and the film, the fear of a Nazi resurgence had given way to the Cold War with Communist Russia and the "space race." In both novel and film, however, Heinlein's patriotism displays American heroes working "for the benefit of all mankind."

CHAPTER BIBLIOGRAPHY

Film References

Goodwin, Michael. "Heinlein on Film: *Destination Moon*." *Omni's Screen Flights/Screen Fantasies*. Ed. Danny Peary. Garden City, NY: Dolphin-Doubleday, 1984, pp. 102–06.

Warren, Bill. "*Destination Moon*." *Keep Watching the Skies! American Science Fiction Movies of the Fifties: Volume 1, 1950–1957*. Jefferson, NC: McFarland, 1982, pp. 2–6.

Film Reviews

Commonweal 52, 21 July 1950: 367.
Holiday 10 (Nov. 1951): 26.
Life 28, 24 April 1950: 107–10.
New Republic 123, 10 July 1950: 22.
New York Times Magazine, 19 Feb. 1950: 46–7.
Newsweek 36, 10 July 1950: 86.
Scholastic 57, 20 Sept. 1950: 38.
Time 56, 10 July 1950: 76.

Novel References

Franklin, H. Bruce. *Robert A. Heinlein: America as Science Fiction*. New York: Oxford University Press, 1980.

Heinlein, Robert A. *Rocket Ship Galileo*. New York: Charles Scribner's Sons, 1947; New York: Ballantine, 1977.

Panshin, Alexei. *Heinlein in Dimension*. Chicago: Advent, 1969.

Novel Reviews

Atlantic 180 (Dec. 1947): 148.
Booklist 44, 15 Dec. 1947: 155.
Kirkus Reviews 15, 1 Nov. 1947: 602.
New Yorker 23, 6 Dec. 1947: 156.

CHAPTER 4

When Worlds Collide

- Paramount (USA), 1951, color, 81 minutes
- **Credits:** *Producer*, George Pal; *director*, Rudolph Maté; *screenplay*, Sydney Boehm, based on the novel by Edwin Balmer and Philip Wylie; *cinematographers*, John F. Seltz and W. Howard Greene; *special effects*, Gordon Jennings and Harry Barndollar; *technical advisor*, Chesley Bonestell; *music*, Leith Stevens
- **Cast:** Richard Derr (Dave Randall), Barbara Rush (Joyce Hendron), Peter Hanson (Dr. Tony Drake), John Hoyt (Sydney Stanton), and Larry Keating (Dr. Hendron)
- **Distributors:** *16 mm*—Films, Inc., 35 South West St., Mount Vernon, NY 10550, (800) 223-6246; *Videotape*—Paramount Home Video, 5555 Melrose Avenue, Hollywood, CA 90038

PLOT SUMMARY

A private pilot, Dave Randall, is hired for $1,500 to carry a black box from a South African observatory to a famous American astronomer, Dr. Hendron. When he arrives at U.S. Customs, he meets Dr. Hendron's daughter, Joyce, who rushes him to her father's laboratory. There he learns that the black box contains photographs and calculations of the path of a star, Bellus, and its planet, Zyra. Using a Differential Analyzer, the Hendrons confirm the path predicted by the South African observatory. In about eight months Zyra will pass close to the Earth, causing massive tidal waves and earthquakes. Nineteen days later the Earth will suffer a head-on collision with Bellus and will be destroyed. Randall meets Joyce Hendron's boyfriend, Dr. Tony Drake; they are soon competing for her affections.

Meanwhile, Dr. Hendron releases his findings and attends a meeting at the United Nations, at which he urges all the nations to build spaceships to carry some people to the planet Zyra after it passes the Earth so that the human race will survive. A number of other scientists ridicule his conclusions. He cannot get financial help to construct spaceships from either the United Nations or the government of the United States. Two private businessmen do help him by renting a construction site and purchasing some of the needed equipment; but more money is needed in order to complete the project. A wealthy but ruthless businessman, Sydney Stanton, then agrees to provide the needed money in exchange for a seat on the spaceship.

About 600 workers, many of whom are university students, are enlisted to build the spaceship. Only 44 persons can be saved in the ship, which must also carry livestock, supplies, and machinery. The ship will take-off by going down a large ramp on a rocket sled and finally turning on its own rockets as it ascends.

Three months before the near-collision with Zyra, the authorities finally acknowledge the coming disaster. People are moved inland to save them from the tidal waves that will be caused by Zyra. The construction site is badly damaged when Zyra passes the Earth, but the ship is saved. We see destruction take place elsewhere on a massive scale. Randall and Drake fly relief supplies to a nearby camp and pick up a little boy stranded on a rooftop.

Dr. Hendron announces that there will be a lottery to determine who boards the spaceship for the flight to Zyra. Everyone selects a number in the lottery with the exception of Dr. Hendron and his daughter, Stanton, Drake, the boy, another key scientist, and Randall, all of whom have guaranteed seats. However, Randall refuses his place, saying that he isn't needed on the new world. Those chosen by the lottery are to be announced just before the take-off.

The spaceship is completed in the nick of time. Drake changes Randall's mind by telling him that the scientist who was scheduled to pilot the spaceship has a bad heart and is not likely to survive the acceleration during take-off. Randall then agrees to go.

After the winners are announced, the losers riot. Dr. Hendron remains on Earth and forcibly prevents Stanton from entering the spaceship. Their places are taken by another worker and the little boy. The spaceship successfully takes off, the Earth is destroyed by Bellus, and Randall lands the ship on Zyra. The planet has a breathable atmosphere, snow, and vegetation. The survivors of Earth set out to build a new society.

Special Effects.   They are excellent; George Pal is at his best. There is excellent model work and matte work. Only the background on Zyra looks unrealistic.

SCIENTIFIC PRINCIPLES RELATED TO THE FILM

Refer to the discussions of gravity and momentum in Chapter 3, pages 27–31.

SCIENTIFIC COMMENTARY

Astronomy. There is an inconsistency between the statement that Bellus and Zyra had moved 1 million miles in two weeks and the statement that they traverse the 3 billion miles separating them from Earth in less than a year. If they are moving at the rate of 1 million miles per two weeks, it will take 6,000 weeks (or about 120 years) to reach the Earth.

• Bellus is described as being a "giant" star that is a dozen times larger than the Earth (see Table 4.1). The radius of Bellus is about one-tenth (.1) that of our Sun, and since volume is proportional to the cube of the radius of a body, its volume would be about one-thousandth (.001) of our Sun's volume, that is, similar to the volume, and probably the mass, of Jupiter. That mass is too small to produce the gravitational attraction in a massive body that would raise the temperature sufficiently at the center of the body to ignite the thermonuclear reaction that powers every sun. In short, Bellus does not have the mass (about .1 that of our Sun) needed to become a star. (See also the discussion of this point in Chapter 11, under *2010.*)

Computers. The Differential Analyzer is probably a crude computer that can calculate the future path of an object from a set of positions versus time of the object.

Astronomy. It is hard to believe that nearly all other astronomers would have reached conclusions different from that of Dr. Hendron about the future paths of Bellus and Zyra.

TABLE 4.1.   Diameter and Mass of Selected Bodies

Body	Mean diameter (miles)	Mass as multiple of Earth's
Sun	866,000	330,000
Jupiter	88,000	318
Earth	7,900	1
Bellus	95,000	300–400?

Spaceships.　　Building a spaceship for interplanetary travel would take many more workers than the 600 described in the movie and would certainly take longer than eight months to complete. The much smaller Apollo spaceships, which landed our astronauts on the Moon, took billions of dollars to build, not the millions mentioned in the film.

• In comparison with our Apollo spaceships, the spaceship in the film is much larger than necessary for the people and animals it is to carry to Zyra. It is 400 feet long and, perhaps, 80 feet in diameter. Its hull appears to be at least a foot thick. If these dimensions are correct, the ship would contain about 90,000 cubic feet of metal. If aluminum was used in the construction, it would weigh about 15 million pounds, or about 7,500 tons! The 7,000 pounds that represent the weight of the passengers is minuscule in comparison. The ship is a one-stage rocket. Thus the entire 15 million pounds of metal would have to be slowed down from its speed of 36,000 miles per hour in outer space in order to land on Zyra. Since the gravitational attraction of Zyra is about the same as that on Earth, it is doubtful that only $1/4$ of the total fuel in the spaceship could slow it sufficiently to land. Its fins are so small that they probably would not slow the spaceship appreciably during the landing. In comparison, our space shuttle, which lands like an aircraft, has much larger wings in order to glide through the atmosphere, to slow down, and to land.

• The launching ramp pictured in the film is similar to those used by the Russians for their early space flights. However, the downward portion of the ramp is only 3,000 feet long, which is relatively short in comparison to the 400-foot-long spaceship.

Gravity.　　The gravitational pull of Zyra, which is about the same size as the Earth and probably has a nearly identical mass, is much larger than that of the Moon. Yet the Moon is the main cause of the daily tides on Earth. Thus Zyra would cause giant tidal waves if it came very close to the Earth. However, it would not be likely to cause earthquakes and volcanoes unless it passed as close to the Earth as the Moon does. In that case, it might well affect the orbit of our Moon, but the picture does not mention this. Note that the Moon has only $1/81$ the mass of the Earth (or presumably of Zyra). Thus Zyra would exert 81 times the gravitational pull of the Moon on the Earth if they were both the same distance from the Earth.

Astronomy.　　Bellus does not look like a sun in the close-up view that we have of it. Rather, it appears to be a reddish planet.

When Worlds Collide: The spaceship accelerates going down its take-off ramp. (Photo: Museum of Modern Art/Film Stills Archive. Courtesy of Paramount Pictures.)

Momentum.   The spaceship changes its orientation in outer space solely by firing its rear rockets. But in order to change the orientation and/or direction of the rocket, rockets would have to be fired in the direction opposite to the change desired, that is, from the sides or front of the spaceship.

Astronomy.   Zyra is the same size as Earth and apparently has the same gravitational attraction at its surface. In addition, there is a breathable atmosphere, ice, and vegetation. As the scientists in the film said, this happy state of affairs is unlikely.

CLASSROOM ACTIVITIES

Exercises to Extend Learning

1. According to the film, how fast are Bellus and Zyra moving toward the Earth? How far away from the Earth are they reported to be at the beginning of the film? Calculate how long it will take them to reach

the Earth from this initial position and compare this calculation with that reported in the film.

2. What is the Differential Analyzer?

3. How many workers are building the spaceship? How long do they have to build the spaceship? What is the approximate length and diameter of the spaceship? If the hull of the spaceship is one-foot thick, how many cubic feet of metal does the spaceship contain? Would the weight of this metal be much greater than the weight of the 44 passengers?

4. Does Bellus look like a sun in the close-up view of it?

5. How does the spaceship change its orientation in outer space? In reality, could the change of a spaceship's orientation be accomplished as depicted in the film?

6. What is the size of the planet Zyra relative to the planet Earth?

Topics for Further Discussion

Astronomy.   What will happen to Zyra as Bellus moves out of our solar system? Since our Sun has a much greater mass than Bellus, might its gravitational attraction cause Bellus and/or Zyra to go into orbit like any other planet in our solar system? If both Bellus and Zyra stayed in our solar system, might the surface temperature on Zyra, due to two suns, become too high to sustain life?

Population Genetics.   Should more women than men have been chosen for the flight to Zyra? Should the selection process have guaranteed that at least some specialists, such as veterinarians and biologists, were included among those going to Zyra? Should Dr. Hendron have planned for a more diverse gene pool among his planetary pioneers? Does Dr. Hendron's approach to the selection constitute eugenics?

Sociology.   Is it likely that the camp would have expended time and energy delivering medical supplies in the surrounding area, after Zyra passed the Earth, when they were behind schedule in the construction of the spaceship? Would Dr. Hendron and the others have been concerned about revealing their existence to survivors in the area because of fear that the survivors might attack the camp? Compare the camp to a bomb shelter after a nuclear attack.

• Assuming that Dr. Hendron's goal was to maximize the chances that some would survive the destruction of Earth, did he act properly in publicly announcing the end of the world? Would he have had a better chance of success by approaching only government officials and some wealthy businessmen *in secret*?

Sexism. The film depicts all engineers as being males and all the technicians as females. Is this a sexist representation?

Literature. What biblical references and analogies are there in the film?

Astronomy. Is it likely that astronomers would not have been able to plot the course of Bellus accurately until it was only 3 billion miles away, that is, near the edge of our solar system? It is, after all, a star that should easily be visible thousands of times further away.

Biology. What would you have taken on the spaceship? Discuss explicitly what kinds of animals, insects, plants, seeds, and medicines you would take. Could we recreate an Earthlike ecosystem or would we have to adapt to Zyra's environment?

Technology. What kinds of computer hardware and software would you take? What types of energy sources (solar, nuclear, etc.) would you take? What tools and clothing would be most useful? Would you take weapons, and if so, what types?

Sociology. Read the sequel novel by Edwin Balmer and Philip Wylie, *After Worlds Collide*. This describes the interactions between the colonies established by several different countries on Zyra.

Literary Commentary

The film version of *When Worlds Collide* has been greatly sentimentalized. The love triangle among Joyce Hendron, Dave Randall, and Tony Drake receives more attention than the collision, floods, earthquakes, or even the ship's construction. The Hendron group also expends valuable time and resources on rescue missions to flood victims, saving children and puppies, and allowing the stereotyped villain, Stanton, to present utterly selfish views so that they can be refuted by the utterly noble Hendron.

In contrast, the 1933 novel, *When Worlds Collide*, by Edwin Balmer and Philip Wylie, is more objective, dispassionate, and credible. The novel opens, as the film does, with Dave transporting photographic plates to Hendron in New York. However, these plates are merely final confirmation of the imminent disaster from the gas giant, Bronson Alpha (Bellus in the film), and of possible salvation on Bronson Beta (Zyra).

Hendron's daughter Eve, who is engaged to stockbroker Tony Drake (an M.D. in the film), works as her father's assistant with calculations. Hendron holds a press conference to issue a statement on behalf of "The League of Last Days," an organization of the world's astronomers, to warn the world of the coming disaster. He also forbids the marriage of Eve and Tony because the League of Last Days will attempt to build a spaceship to reach Bronson Beta. There marriage will no longer exist because the gene pool will be so small that the women must bear children to several men.

Hendron, Drake, and their colleagues are wealthy men who do their own financing for a site, equipment, and construction in Michigan. They believe it will remain stable during the earthquakes, volcanic eruptions, and tidal waves caused by the first pass of the Bronson bodies, which will occur in about a year. Drake travels to various scientific establishments and universities recruiting the most promising scientists for the team, a job done by Randall and Joyce in the film. During this time, the United States government undertakes the massive task of evacuating most of the seaboard population to the mountains and plains of the Midwest, not merely because the area may escape significant damage from tidal waves and earthquakes, but also because it is the only part of the continent capable of providing sufficient food for such a large number of people.

The government believes that the Bronson bodies will cause enormous damage, then pass on into interstellar space. They do not believe Hendron's statement that the Bronson bodies will make a second pass about a year later and actually destroy the Earth. The first pass virtually destroys the resettlement areas in the Midwest as well as coastal cities subject to 700-foot tides. Bronson Alpha collides with and destroys the Moon.

The Hendron camp area is geologically stable, however, and the scientists there feverishly continue construction of the ship before the Bronson bodies return. The ship will have atomic power, and the major problem continues to be finding an alloy that will withstand the enormous temperatures produced by the engine. On an exploratory flight to estimate the extent of the damage and to see whether any government or civilization survives, Randall discovers an unknown metal thrown up by volcanic action. This proves to be the solution, and enough of it exists to build a second ship. Construction on the second ship begins immediately.

An enormous band of destitute survivors from the surrounding area gathers to attack the camp, killing many of Hendron's group. They are ultimately defeated only by lifting the ship in order to use the atomic blast of its engine against the attackers. This weakens an otherwise strong plot, because the novel contains no thought of residual radiation and its effects on the survivors. They continue to consider the needs of survival on Bronson Beta, carefully considering weight limitations against the need for food, water, equipment, seeds, and animals. They believe that vegetation reproducing by spores may yet survive on Bronson Beta and that Earth vegetation and animals may also be able to survive. Their telescopes have shown them the remains of cities on the planet.

They complete the second ship in time, and the night before take-off Eve and Drake, on a last walk around the camp, hear crying. They discover a boy and a girl standing outside the perimeter fence. The children tell them that their father left them there, saying that someone would find them and take care of them. With so many of Hendron's group killed in the earlier attack, and with the second ship, taking the children is no problem.

The novel concludes with a French scientist arriving in the nick of time to board Hendron's ship. The two ships then leave and, from space, the survivors watch the collision of Bronson Alpha with Earth. Only Hendron's ship lands on Bronson Beta. Tony and Eve discover a lichen-like plant surviving, and they go off hand-in-hand to investigate one of the cities still standing from when the planet was previously inhabited.

CHAPTER BIBLIOGRAPHY

Film References

Warren, Bill. "*When Worlds Collide.*" *Keep Watching the Skies! American Science Fiction Movies of the Fifties: Volume One, 1950–1957*. Jefferson, NC: McFarland, 1982, pp. 58–66.

Film Reviews

Catholic World 174 (Nov. 1951): 144.
Christian Century 68, 12 Dec. 1951: 1447.
Holiday 10 (Nov. 1951): 25.
Newsweek 39, 3 Mar. 1952: 88.
Saturday Review of Literature 34, 10 Nov. 1951: 28.
Scholastic 59, 28 Nov. 1951: 22.
Time 58, 12 Nov. 1951: 114 ff.

Novel References

Balmer, Edwin and Wylie, Philip. *When Worlds Collide*. Philadelphia: J. B. Lippincott, 1933; New York: Warner Books, 1962.

Bendau, Clifford P. *"When Worlds Collide* and *After Worlds Collide." Survey of Science Fiction Literature.* Ed. Frank N. Magill. Englewood Cliffs, NJ: Salem, 1979, pp. 2463–68.
Keefer, Truman Frederick. *Philip Wylie.* Twayne American Authors. Boston: Twayne, 1977.

Novel Reviews

Books, 5 Mar. 1933: 1.
New Republic 74, 15 Mar. 1933: 138.
New York Times, 12 Mar. 1933: 7.
Times Literary Supplement, 7 Dec. 1933: 880.

CHAPTER 5

The Day the Earth Stood Still

- 20th Century Fox (USA), 1951, black and white, 92 minutes
- **Credits:** *Producer*, Julian Blaustein; *director*, Robert Wise; *screenplay*, Edmund H. North, based on "Farewell to the Master," by Harry Bates; *cinematographer*, Leo Tover; *special effects*, Fred Sersen; *music*, Bernard Herrmann
- **Cast:** Michael Rennie (Klaatu), Patricia Neal (Helen Benson), Hugh Marlow (Tom Stevens), Sam Jaffe (Professor Barnhardt), Billy Gray (Bobby Benson), and Gort the Robot
- **Distributors:** *16 mm* — Films, Inc., 35 South West St., Mt. Vernon, NY 10550, (800) 223-6246; *Videotape* — 20th Century Fox Video, Industrial Park Drive, Farmington Hills, MI 48024

PLOT SUMMARY

An alien spaceship is monitored on radar as it travels completely around the globe. The spaceship lands in Washington, D.C., and it is surrounded by the military. A couple of hours after it lands, an opening appears in the side of the ship and an emissary, Klaatu, walks from it. He is shot in the arm as he extends an object that the military fears is a weapon. Actually it is a device by which our president can see life as it exists on other planets. A giant robot, Gort, emerges after the emissary is shot. The robot emits a beam that disintegrates rifles, artillery pieces, and even tanks. The robot then stands immobile, and the ship reseals itself as Klaatu is taken to Walter Reed Hospital.

After he is treated for his wound, he requests a meeting with the heads of all nations on Earth. A number of them refuse to attend, and Klaatu decides that he needs to understand the people of Earth better before determining a course of action. He then manages to escape and, wearing a stolen suit, goes to a boardinghouse. There he meets Helen Benson, a widow, and her son Bobby.

The next day he is taken by Bobby on a tour of Washington, D.C.,

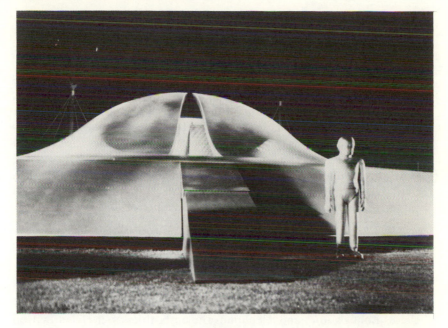

The Day the Earth Stood Still: Gort, the robot, stands guard alongside the alien spaceship. (Photo: Museum of Modern Art/Film Stills Archive. Courtesy of 20th Century-Fox.)

during which Klaatu suggests that he be taken to the home of the smartest man on Earth, Professor Barnhardt.

There, Klaatu modifies a formula that Barnhardt has been working on and leaves his assumed name (Carpenter) and address with Barnhardt's secretary; the professor has Klaatu picked up by the authorities and brought to his office. Only then does he learn that Klaatu is the alien who is being sought by the authorities. When Klaatu tells Barnhardt that the very survival of the human race is at stake, Barnhardt agrees to call a meeting of all the world's leading scientists in two days time. He asks Klaatu to give the world a demonstration that will make humanity realize that the message he brings cannot be ignored. Klaatu promises a spectacular demonstration of power.

Klaatu borrows a flashlight from Bobby that evening and uses it to signal Gort. The robot knocks out its guards and Klaatu reenters the spaceship, unaware that Bobby has followed him. Inside the ship, Klaatu apparently prepares the demonstration for humanity.

Bobby tells his mother and her friend Tom Stevens that the new boarder is the alien, Klaatu. They don't believe him at first; then Stevens finds a diamond in Klaatu's room, and Bobby tells them that Klaatu gave him two diamonds in exchange for $2.

The next morning Klaatu comes to see Helen Benson at her office, reveals his true identity, and asks her to assist him in avoiding the authorities until the meeting that Professor Barnhardt has arranged for that evening is completed. She agrees to help him when she realizes the consequences if he fails in his mission. They are trapped together for half an hour in an elevator when "electricity has been neutralized all over the world," according to Klaatu. Elevators, cars, and trains all stop. However, electricity continues to function in airplanes, hospitals, and other vital locations. This demonstration of the awesome power of the aliens panics the authorities. Since Gort remains immobile throughout the worldwide electricity shutoff, the robot is assumed to be uninvolved in these events, and Klaatu is blamed for them instead. The military vows to apprehend him, dead or alive.

Meanwhile, Stevens is told by three jewelers that they have never seen a diamond like the one he found in Klaatu's bedroom. Stevens now believes Bobby's story and telephones the authorities after Helen Benson is unable to dissuade him from exposing Klaatu. She rushes to the boardinghouse and picks up Klaatu in a taxi only seconds ahead of the military. They are pursued, and Klaatu warns her that if he is killed she must prevent Gort from destroying the world by saying to the robot "Klaatu barada nikto." When the military does shoot Klaatu and he dies, Benson hurries to the spaceship. The robot apparently knows that Klaatu has been killed, because it melts the "KL 93" plastic casing designed to imprison it and disintegrates its guards. After Benson delivers her message, the robot carries her into the ship and then brings back Klaatu's body. The robot places the body on a device that applies some mysterious radiation to it, and Klaatu awakens. He tells Benson that this device, in some cases, can restore life for a limited period.

They then leave the spaceship, and Klaatu delivers his message to the scientists assembled by Professor Barnhardt. Unless humanity gives up aggression, the robot police force that patrols the planets will destroy Earth. Klaatu and Gort reenter their spaceship, and it flies off.

Special Effects. The special effects are minimal but well done. They include an excellent screen spaceship, both externally and internally, as well as the disintegration of both men and machines by the robot. In addition, a brilliant score utilizing electronic instrumentation was created for the film by Bernard Hermann, and it added much to the sinister mood of this work.

SCIENTIFIC PRINCIPLES RELATED TO THE FILM

Electricity

The universe in which we live is made up of atoms, which contain electrical charges. One may picture an atom as consisting of a dense nucleus, containing protons and neutrons and surrounded by electrons that move about the nucleus in a manner similar to the way planets in our solar system move about the Sun. It is the electrical force between the protons in the nucleus and the electrons in orbit around it that keeps the atom intact. In a neutral atom, there are as many positive protons in the nucleus as there are negative electrons in orbit around the nucleus. Each proton has an identical positive charge of $+1.6 \times 10^{-19}$ coulombs, while each electron has an identical negative charge of -1.6×10^{-19} coulombs. The forces between electrical charges follow very simple rules:

Like electrical charges repel
Unlike electrical charges attract

Thus two protons, each carrying a positive charge, will repel one another, while a proton and an electron, having unlike charges, will attract one another.

In 1785, the French physicist Coulomb determined that the force between two charges, q_1 and q_2, is directly proportional to the product of the charges and inversely proportional to the square of the distance r between the charges: $F = K q_1 q_2 / r^2$ where K is a proportionality constant that depends on the units in which q and r are measured. In this formula, one assumes that the size of the electrical charges is small compared to the distance between them, so that they may be treated as points that have a single unique distance, r, between them. According to Coulomb's formula all charges in the universe interact with all other charges, since only when r becomes infinite does the force between the charges become zero.

Machines operated by electricity involve electrical currents. One can define an electrical current as the amount of charge that passes through a given cross-section of a wire each second. We use the symbol I to represent this current. The unit of current is the ampere, which is defined to be the passage of 1 coulomb of electrical charge per second.

All materials at room temperature or above have a resistance to the passage of an electrical current. For many materials there is a simple relationship between the resistance, R, of the material, the current, I, passing through the material, and the voltage drop, V, across the materi-

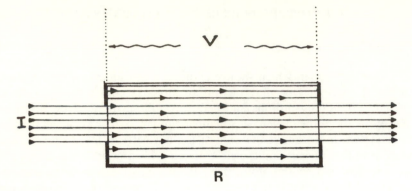

FIGURE 5.1.   The current, *I* (arrows), flowing through a resistor, *R*, that has a voltage difference, *V*, across it.

al. This relationship is called Ohm's Law, $V=IR$; as Figure 5.1 indicates, the potential drop is measured between the extremities of the resistor, R. The units commonly used are volts for V, amperes for I, and ohms for R. The wall sockets in your home probably have an average voltage drop of 110 volts between their prongs. This voltage varies sinusoidally in time and is therefore called an alternating voltage in contrast to a voltage that does not vary sinusoidally with time, such as that from a battery. You can use Ohm's Law to solve for any one of the three symbols if the other two are given. For example, if an air conditioner draws 11 amperes when plugged into the 110-volt wall socket, its internal resistance, $R = 110$ volts/11 amperes = 10 ohms. As another example, if a toaster has an internal resistance of 100 ohms it will draw a current, I, equal to 110 volts/100 ohms = 1.1 amperes when plugged into the 110-volt wall socket.

Some important processes of the human body, notably the contraction of muscles and the conduction of impulses upon cells of the nervous system, depend on creating currents at cell surfaces. When a metal wire carries a current, it does so by the localized movements of electrons. In the body, whose materials are not metallic, currents are created by the movement of ions, particularly positively charged ions.

When a muscle cell is at rest, its membrane is *polarized* (see Figure 5.2a). The cell membrane contains so-called pumps that move sodium ions to the outside of the cell, and since negatively charged ions are excluded from passage through membrane pores, the cell membrane displays a potential difference across the membrane. The membrane is posi-

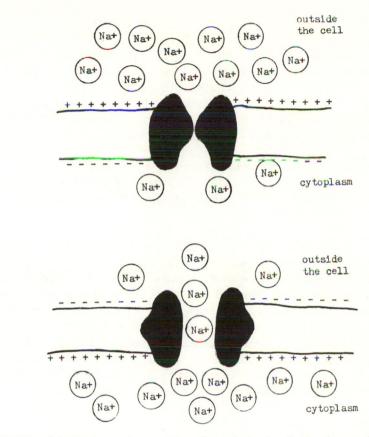

FIGURE 5.2.   (a) Diagram of a portion of a polarized cell membrane; (b) Diagram of a portion of a depolarized cell membrane.

tively charged on the outside and negatively charged on the inside. This potential difference can be measured by electrodes in millivolts. When the stimulus for a muscle cell to contract reaches the cell membrane, it briefly interferes with the sodium pump so that sodium ions diffuse into the cell's interior, thus reducing the membrane potential and *depolarizing* the membrane (see Figure 5.2b). Depolarization spreads over the cell surface and then triggers events leading to contraction by specialized components inside the cell. A similar propagation of depolarization produces the impulses that travel on neurons.

SCIENTIFIC COMMENTARY

Aeronautics.   The alien spaceship is reported to fly at 4,000 miles per hour and at a height of 20,000 feet. This is scientifically possible. In fact, it is not very spectacular today. However, the sonic boom that should accompany anything moving faster than the speed of sound is not heard. The saucer appears to be large, and its exact size can be estimated from the baseball field on which it lands.

Electricity.   Perhaps Gort evaporated the guns and tanks by turning off the electrical forces holding the atoms together. If this was the case, why did the atoms of the rifles disintegrate but not those of the soldiers or their clothing?

Astronomy.   Klaatu stated that he had traveled 250 million miles in five months from another inhabited planet. There are no inhabited planets other than Earth in our solar system. The distance to the nearest star, Alpha Centauri, is about 4.3 light years, an immensely greater distance. Thus no inhabited planet could exist at 250 million miles from Earth.

The average speed at which Klaatu traveled was about 70,000 miles per hour. This is not that much greater than the escape velocity from the Earth of 25,000 miles per hour.

Metallurgy.   The military are unable to pierce the ship's hull with either diamond drills or blow torches. Apparently it and the robot are made of a superstrong material, but we are told nothing further of its properties. Any earthly metal would have been penetrated.

Biology.   The doctors state that Klaatu has the same skeletal structure and internal organs as a human being. Perhaps the human race and Klaatu's are the same. We do not know the composition of his blood or his cell structure. His 130-year life expectancy is not really that different from ours. Humans have lived to that age and, in theory, with better medical techniques the average human might approach that life expectancy. These findings together suggest that Klaatu's cells could be similar to human cells, with some differences in the number of cell generations possibly accounting for a longer life span.

Mechanics.   Klaatu correctly defines inertia, which is the tendency of a body to maintain its state of rest or of uniform motion in a straight line.

Communications. It is preposterous for the film to suggest that only two men would be guarding the robot when Klaatu contacts it with a flashlight in order to activate it and thereby to enter the spaceship. Moreover, any civilization advanced enough to be able to destroy an entire planet could surely provide its representative with an electronic communications device powerful enough to establish contact with the robot over a distance of only a few miles. The device could have been implanted in one of Klaatu's teeth, for example.

Electricity. The selective turning off of electricity on the surface of the entire planet appears to be a physical impossibility. We do not know of any mechanism capable of doing this. Furthermore, if one turned off the forces around all electrons (these are the electrical charges that move down wires in generators, etc.), presumably all of the atoms would collapse and the electrons would fly off in every direction. This would disintegrate the machines and their occupants. Secondly, since electrical forces have an inverse square dependence on distance, it seems unlikely that Gort or the spaceship could turn off the electrical current in a car without turning off the electrical currents in its occupant. Even if the aliens could distinguish between electrical currents produced by electrons alone (as in machinery) and the electrical currents in the human body produced by the flow of charged ions, how could they distinguish among the wires the electrons were flowing down? How could the aliens stop the transmission of radio and television waves in the atmosphere without turning off the currents needed to operate an airplane in that same atmosphere? In short, even if they possessed the power to turn off electrical forces, they could not have achieved the results depicted in the film.

Energy. It is not clear how Gort could reduce Earth to a cinder. The amount of energy needed to blow apart the Earth is immense. Even if the entire alien spaceship were to be converted into pure energy the resulting explosion could not possibly destroy the Earth.

Biology. When Gort picks up Klaatu's body, rigor mortis should have set in, yet the body is limp. We do not know how Gort brought Klaatu back to life. However, if the robot was able to bring him back to life, the damage to his body (and his brain cells) would have had to be largely repaired. If that were the case, why wouldn't Klaatu live out his normal life span?

Communications. Klaatu could have addressed the entire world directly over all radio and television networks. This would have been a far more impressive way of delivering his message.

Energy. Klaatu tells Bobby that the spaceship has an atomic power plant. Presumably this supplies the energy to propel the ship. Yet we do not see rockets emitted from it as it rises from the ground. Unless the ship was able to neutralize the gravitational pull of Earth, it is not clear how it could rise so gently into the air. There is no known way of neutralizing gravity.

CLASSROOM ACTIVITIES

Exercises to Extend Learning

1. How large is the flying saucer?
2. How far did Klaatu state he had traveled? Was his home planet inside or outside of our solar system?
3. What methods did the military use to try to penetrate the ship's hull?
4. How does Klaatu define inertia?
5. How many guards were stationed around the alien robot and spaceship? Does this number seem reasonable to you?
6. How does Klaatu signal to the giant robot?
7. Describe the manner in which electricity was neutralized all over the globe. Where wasn't it neutralized?
8. When the robot picks up Klaatu's body, is the body limp or rigid? Should it have been limp or rigid?
9. How is the alien spaceship powered?
10. Can you think of a more effective way for Klaatu to have delivered his message to the human race than the method he chose?

Topics for Further Discussion

Sociology. Since Klaatu was familiar with the human race from having monitored our radio and television broadcasts, why did he act in a manner to maximize his chances of being killed? He emerges from his spaceship with his face concealed and suddenly pushes forward an object that obviously appeared to be a weapon. On top of that, he is not protected by some kind of body armor, which his technology could have constructed.

• Would the military have released Helen Benson when Klaatu died? It is very unlikely that they would have let her go. If they didn't, presumably Gort would have destroyed the world. This makes Klaatu's leaping from the cab and running away an irrational act. It would have been far better to have surrendered and then summoned the robot, especially in view of his statement that he could be restored to life only for a limited period of time.

Security.   What is the likelihood that Klaatu could have escaped from the hospital?

Crystallography.   Could a jeweler have determined that the diamond found by Mr. Stevens didn't originate on Earth? If so, how?

Political Science.   Compare Klaatu's inability to bring together the heads of all countries to discuss limiting the spread of the arms race to outer space with the difficulties facing us today in achieving an international agreement on this matter.

Aviation.   Compare the speed of the alien spaceship to that of the SST.

Psychology.   Professor Barnhardt did not turn Klaatu over to the military. Was Barnhardt's action based mainly on his faith that Klaatu is friendly or on his curiosity about Klaatu's scientific knowledge?

LITERARY COMMENTARY

Harry Bates's 1940 novelette "Farewell to the Master" bears only superficial resemblance to the film based upon it, as Bates himself has acknowledged. From "Farewell to the Master" the filmmakers have borrowed the spaceship, the fearsome eight-foot robot (Gnut in the story), Klaatu the benign and fully human ambassador, and two concepts: resurrecting the dead and the robot's being the man's superior rather than servant. Otherwise, the novelette and the film are quite different.

In the novelette, the spaceship "materializes" through "relativistic means," but in the film radar tracks its arrival at the relatively slow speed of 4,000 miles per hour. Radar was invented during the interval between the novelette's publication and the film's production. The ship's appearance is the same, a smooth ovoid, and it lands in the same place, Washington, D.C. In both novelette and film, the ship is surrounded by a heavily armed military cordon and a gawking crowd. In the novelette, though, Klaatu is killed by a "madman" from the crowd rather than shot by a nervous soldier and later hunted down and killed. The robot merely freezes in position, and the "Interplanetary Wing of the Smithsonian Museum" is constructed around the robot and the ship, while Klaatu's body is interred in a mausoleum.

Much later a curious reporter, Cliff Sutherland, discovers that the robot has moved. He hides in the museum to spy and discovers that it conducts experiments at night. He hears a mockingbird's song, sees the bird fly and drop to the floor dead. He hears animal sounds, sees a gorilla rush from the ship, wrestle with the robot, then drop to its knees and die. Later he hears a human voice and sees a man come from the ship. He also dies, apparently uninjured. When Sutherland reports these events to the "Continental Bureau of Investigation," Gnut is encased in "glasstex" to immobilize him. He later melts the plastic as he does the KL 93 in the film. He continues his experiment.

For his experiment, Gnut has created a device that can use a recording to re-create the living creature that has made the sounds recorded. He even re-creates Klaatu briefly, although Klaatu tells the reporter that he, too, is dying. The theory is that each body possesses a distinctive sound; from that sound, as re-created by a recording, the body can be re-created. If the recording is flawed, the re-created body will be flawed, so Klaatu, like the mockingbird and the gorilla, is flawed and dying. Klaatu dies again, in Sutherland's arms.

The novelette contains nothing of the threat to humanity that the film possesses, and none of the strange diamonds, celestial mechanics, or stopping of electrical power. When Klaatu dies the second time, Sutherland begs the robot to tell its masters that his death was the work of a madman, that everyone on Earth regrets it. The robot then tells Sutherland that "I am the master," and the ship leaves.

Compared to the film, the novelette has a slight plot and few characters, all stereotypical. The only suspense derives from Sutherland's trying to discover what Gnut's experiments are for. The motivation for the ship's arrival is never clarified, nor is the motivation for its departure. A significant change for the better occurs in the image of the robot and in its character. In the story, Gnut has "two red eyes," but only the discovery of his midnight movements makes him at all interesting. He is bland and benevolent. In the film, Gort's visor and ray, his destruction of weapons, and his assistance to Klaatu provide him with an air of menacing omnipotence appropriate to his role of judge and potential executioner.

CHAPTER BIBLIOGRAPHY

Film References

Warren, Bill. *"The Day the Earth Stood Still." Keep Watching the Skies! American Science Fiction Movies of the Fifties: Volume 1, 1950–1957.* Jefferson, NC: McFarland, 1982, pp. 19–28.

Film Reviews

Christian Century 68, 31 Oct. 1951: 1263.
Nation 174, 5 Jan. 1952: 19.
New Yorker 27, 22 Sept. 1951: 107.
Newsweek 38, 1 Oct. 1951: 90.
Saturday Review of Literature 34, 6 Oct. 1951: 35.
Scholastic 59, 31 Oct. 1951: 30.
Time 58, 1 Oct. 1951: 98 ff.

Novelette References

Bates, Harry. "Farewell to the Master." *Astounding Science Fiction* (Oct. 1940): 58 ff.; rpt. *They Came from Outer Space: 12 Classic Science Fiction Tales That Became Major Motion Pictures.* Ed. Jim Wynorski. Garden City, NY: Doubleday, 1980, pp. 93–132.

CHAPTER 6

Them!

- Warner Brothers (USA), 1954, black and white, 93 minutes
- **Credits:** *Producer*, David Weisbart; *director*, Gordon Douglas; *screenplay*, Ted Sherdeman, based on a story by George Worthington Yates; *cinematographer*, Sid Hickox; *special effects*, Ralph Ayers; *special sound effects*, William Mueller and Francis J. Scheid
- **Cast:** James Whitmore (Sergeant Ben Petersen), James Arness (Robert Graham), Joan Weldon (Dr. Patricia Medford), and Edmund Gwenn (Dr. Medford)
- **Distributors:** *16 mm* — Films, Inc., 35 South West St., Mount Vernon, NY 10550, (800) 223-6246; *Videotape* — Warner Home Video, 4000 Warner Blvd., Burbank, CA 91522

PLOT SUMMARY

As the movie opens, a little girl is wandering aimlessly in the desert. She is rescued by Sergeant Ben Petersen and taken to a trailer to see if the occupants know her. Upon arrival at the trailer, they find one of its sides pulled apart and sugar cubes scattered about; the occupants are nowhere to be found. No money has been taken. The little girl is taken to a hospital, and Petersen and another patrolman stop at a country store. There they find the owner dead and the place in a shambles. Money is still in the cash register. The other patrolman is left on guard while Petersen goes to the hospital. The patrolman hears a strange, rapidly pulsating, high-pitched sound, goes outside to investigate, screams, and fires his gun.

Local police authorities are outraged by the disappearance of the patrolman and call in the FBI for assistance. Special Agent Robert Graham arrives as the coroner informs the police that the store owner not only has a broken back and skull; his body contains enough formic acid to kill 20 men. The cast of an imprint found near the trailer is sent to FBI headquarters for identification.

Washington sends two scientists (Dr. Medford and his daughter, Patricia, the younger Dr. Medford) to the scene. They are experts on insects;

the older Dr. Medford is a renowned myrmecologist. At the hospital they shock the little girl out of her trance-like state by having her smell formic acid. The girl screams, "Them!"

The scientists then return to the trailer site and encounter a giant ant. The sidearms of Petersen and Graham disable the ant, but it takes a submachine gun to kill it. Dr. Medford speculates that the atomic bomb exploded nine years earlier, in 1945, at White Sands, New Mexico, may have caused mutations in the desert ants to produce these giants. The authorities then search for the nest of these giant ants. When it is located, Dr. Medford advises the authorities to attack it during the day because the heat tends to drive the ants inside the nest and thus none will escape. Cyanide gas grenades are hurled into the tunnel entrance of the nest. Graham, Petersen, and Patricia Medford, wearing gas masks and armed with a flamethrower and machine gun, enter the nest itself. After surviving an attack by some ants that had been sealed off from the gas, they reach the queen ant's chamber. To their horror, they discover that two new queens have hatched and flown away from the nest.

Them! Dr. Patricia Medford is menaced by a giant ant in the New Mexican desert. (Photo: Museum of Modern Art/Film Stills Archive. Courtesy of Warner Bros.)

Them! Robert Graham, Dr. Patricia Medford, and Sergeant Ben Peterson enter the giant ant nest beneath the New Mexican desert. (Photo: Museum of Modern Art/Film Stills Archive. Courtesy of Warner Bros.)

The federal authorities begin a nationwide hunt for the escaped queens. All stories about UFOs, flying insects, and other strange events are reported to Washington. The group visits a private pilot who claims to have seen UFOs shaped like ants. They are convinced that he has seen one of the queens and her male consorts. The pilot has been detained in a mental institution, and Graham ensures that he will not spread the story when he instructs a physician to keep him there until the government determines that the pilot is well! This is part of the general government cover-up designed to avoid a nationwide panic.

Finally, one of the queens turns up on board a ship at sea. It apparently entered through an open hold while the ship was docked at a Mexican port. The entire ship is infested with the giant ants, and naval gunfire sinks it.

The second queen ant has apparently landed in Los Angeles, since 40 tons of sugar have been stolen from a boxcar. Graham and Petersen travel to Los Angeles to investigate the theft. A father, dead and missing one arm, is found in his car, but his children have disappeared. With information from a drunk, Graham and Petersen find the model plane that the two boys were flying near the entrance to a 700-mile-long sewer system.

The authorities finally announce the existence of the giant ants and prepare for a major military operation against them. They reject the idea of pouring gasoline into the sewers and setting them afire because Dr. Medford cautions that they must know whether any new queens have escaped this new nest and they are concerned about saving the boys. They therefore send in a large number of patrols. Petersen's unit locates the missing boys in the nest, and he dies while saving both children. The military then converges on the nest, and there is a furious battle at virtually point-blank range against the ants. Only after all of the worker ants are killed do the troops enter the queen's chamber. They find that all the newly hatched queens are still in the nest. These are destroyed, and humanity is saved. The picture ends with a somber question: If the first bomb explosion produced the giant ants, what did all of the subsequent explosions lead to?

Special Effects. The special effects are excellent, including outstanding miniaturized photography, model work, and faultless matte work.

SCIENTIFIC PRINCIPLES RELATED TO THE FILM

Nuclear Physics

In order to understand the action of radiation of living things, one must first have some knowledge of the structure of atoms. Each atom consists of a nucleus, containing protons and neutrons, and a cloud of electrons surrounding the nucleus. The properties of these elementary particles are summarized in Table 6.1.

Each element in nature, such as hydrogen, helium, and so forth, is

TABLE 6.1.   Properties of Elementary Particles

Particle	Mass (kg)	Charge (coulomb)
proton	1.6726×10^{-27}	$+1.6 \times 10^{-19}$
neutron	1.6750×10^{-27}	0
electron	9.1095×10^{-31}	-1.6×10^{-19}

characterized by a specific number of protons in the nucleus. Isotopes of a given element have the same number of protons but different numbers of neutrons. Scientists use a shorthand notation to describe a given nucleus. The subscript to the left of the symbol representing the element gives the number of protons in the nucleus, while the superscript to the right of the symbol gives the number of protons and neutrons in the nucleus. Thus, $_{92}U^{235}$ represents an isotope of uranium that has 92 protons and $235-92=143$ neutrons in its nucleus. Sometimes the subscript is omitted, since all uranium nuclei have 92 protons. Thus U^{235} is another way of writing $_{92}U^{235}$.

Since like electrical charges repel, there must be another force to hold the positively charged protons together in the nucleus. This is called the nuclear force and is attractive. This force is identical between two protons, two neutrons, or a proton and a neutron. However, nuclear forces extend only over very short distances, on the order of 10^{-15} meters, which is about 100,000 times smaller than the size of an atom.

When a slow neutron strikes a U^{235} nucleus, the nucleus disintegrates. This is an example of nuclear fission, which occurs when a large nucleus is broken into two or more nuclei. If the combined masses of the smaller nuclei are less than that of the parent nucleus, the mass loss is converted into pure energy. In U^{235}, the byproduct of a disintegration includes the release of two or three additional neutrons, which may in turn strike other U^{235} nuclei, causing them to disintegrate with the release of yet more neutrons and more energy. As Figure 6.1 illustrates, this leads to a chain reaction. If the size of the sample of U^{235} is too small, the neutrons will escape without striking other U^{235} and a chain reaction will not occur. On the other hand, if there is a sufficient number of U^{235} atoms, an amount called the critical mass, the chain reaction occurs in a small fraction of a second and results in an explosion—an atomic bomb.

Since the amount of U^{235} needed to build an atomic bomb is quite small (the uranium used in the Hiroshima bomb was about the size of a baseball), there is concern that terrorists could steal enough fissionable material to build a suitcase-sized atomic bomb. One simply needs an explosive device that will bring together subcritical masses of the fissionable material in the proper geometric configuration for the explosion to occur.

In addition to nuclear fission as a process of converting mass to energy, there is nuclear fusion. In this process four hydrogen nuclei are combined into one helium nucleus, and the difference in mass between the two is converted into energy. This is the process that occurs in the Sun. It is difficult to initiate, since it only occurs at temperatures on the order of millions of degrees. Humans have been able to achieve these

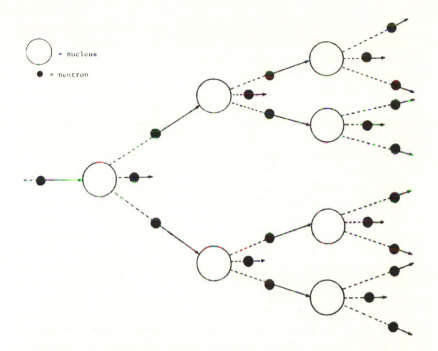

FIGURE 6.1.   A chain reaction. The small solid spheres are neutrons, which bombard fissionable nuclei. Each middle neutron is depicted as leaving the sample without interacting with a nucleus.

temperatures by exploding an atomic bomb. Thus the thermonuclear, or hydrogen, bomb has an atomic bomb as its trigger. There is no limit to the size or explosive power of a hydrogen bomb, because its nuclear fuel is noncombustible until ignited by the explosion of an atomic bomb. The largest hydrogen bomb exploded to date had the explosive power equivalent to 68 million tons of TNT!

Radiation

When nuclei disintegrate, they emit various kinds of radiation. Among the particles emitted are an alpha-particle, which is a helium nucleus consisting of two protons and two neutrons; a beta-particle, which is a high speed electron; a gamma-ray, which is a high-energy bundle of electromagnetic energy; an x-ray, which is a lower-energy bundle of electromagnetic radiation; and both fast and slow neutrons.

Radiation Effects on Humans.   In order to discuss the effects of radiation, we must define the standard unit of radiation dosage. It is called the REM, the abbreviation for Roentgen Equivalent Man. This unit of radiation has already taken account of the fact that different kinds of radiation have different effects on humans. For example, a given amount of energy absorbed from neutrons will do more biological damage than the same amount of energy absorbed from x-rays.

Mutations may be caused by radiation exposure. X-rays and gamma-rays cause mutations with frequencies that depend mainly on the dose rate, while electrons and alpha-particles cause mutations in a dose-dependent fashion. The effects of radiation may be more severe when a given amount of radiation is received at one time rather than in small amounts over a long period. Table 6.2 lists the effects of a single exposure to a given level of radiation.

It is generally agreed that there is no level of radiation exposure at which there is zero damage to human beings. The question is one of balancing the benefits of radiation, such as nuclear power plants, medical x-rays, tracer studies of the circulatory system, and cancer therapy, against the dangers of radiation exposure. Some scientists suggest that on average the general population should not have a whole body exposure to radiation that exceeds 0.5 REM per year.

Various estimates have been made as to the shortening of the lifespan due to radiation exposure. Some estimates suggest that the lifespan is shortened between 1 and 10 days per REM for a one-shot exposure. Another estimate equated a 1-REM single dose exposure to smoking 143 cigarettes.

Let us next consider Table 6.3, which lists typical radiation-dose levels of the whole body from "normal" radiation sources. In toto the

TABLE 6.2.   Effects of Exposure to Radiation

Exposure level (REMs)	Effects
1	No detectable body change
10	Blood change barely detectable
100	Blood changes detectable, mild nausea, some damage to bone marrow, complete recovery expected
200	Vomiting, fatigue, more substantial blood changes, complete recovery expected
400	Above effects plus infection, bleeding, temporary sterility. Approximately 50% die in 60 days
600–800	Approximately 80–100% die within 60 days. Effects include damage to the central nervous system
5,000	Rapid death due to damage of central nervous system

TABLE 6.3.   Exposure Levels from Common Radiation Sources

Radiation source	Exposure level
Medical X-rays	0.1 REMs per year
Weapons fallout	0.001–0.006 REMs per year
TV screen	0.001 REMs per year
Natural radioactivity	0.015–0.140 REMs per year
Cosmic rays	0.035 REMs per year (sea level)
	0.060 REMs per year (5,000 feet elevation)

average American is subjected to about 0.2 REMs per year, although the amount of radiation a given individual receives may vary substantially, depending upon such factors as the number of medical x-rays taken or where a person lives. Although nuclear power plants presently do not contribute appreciably to the national exposure level, there is concern that as they proliferate their operation will contribute appreciably to the radiation level, and there is, of course, the danger of a nuclear accident or sabotage.

Mutagenicity.   In addition to the biological effects of radiation that are evident immediately, another kind of biological result of exposure to radiation is the production of mutant cells. Radiation reaching a body cell may permanently alter the chemical structure of its DNA such that when the cell divides, its daughter cells are not duplicates of it, as would normally be the case. Such a change in the genetic character of a cell is called a mutation. An agent that causes mutation is called a mutagen. Mutations may cause no harmful changes in cellular structure and function and thus be of no consequence. However, mutations also may alter a cell such that it no longer performs its bodily chores and even takes on a new set of characteristics that might be detrimental to the body. One such change would be the transition from normal cell to cancer cell. Cancer cells proliferate wildly, causing tumors. Moreover, they may spread from an original tumor site to new body locations. Hence the mutation of a single cell can lead to the occurrence of cancer at multiple body sites, a process called metastasis. Survivors of the atomic bombs detonated by the United States in Japan have high incidences of cancer, especially leukemia, a fact that is consistent with mutation by radiation inducing the cancers.

Mutation may also interfere with embryonic development to cause death, anatomic abnormalities, or physiological malfunction in the embryo. Agents that produce such activity are called teratogens. When radiation causes mutation in germ cells or in cells of a developing embryo, it may produce teratogenic changes. Cells that are reproducing are most susceptible to radiation, since the duplication of the genetic information contained in the nuclear DNA requires that it be stripped of its associated proteins and unwound. The blood-cell–forming stem cells of the bone marrow are an example of a cell population that divides throughout life. The DNA of developing blood cells has a much greater chance of being mutated than does the DNA in cell populations that are not dividing. This generalization is borne out by the high rates of leukemia in Japanese survivors of the A-bombs and the fact that the first clinical symptoms of radiation involve blood abnormalities.

Another susceptible population of dividing cells is the spermatogonia of the testis. These cells divide constantly to produce cells that mature into sperm cells. The testis produces many millions of cells a year after puberty in humans; one human ejaculate of 3 or 4 milliliters contains about 400 million sperm cells. Substantial doses of radiation are known to cause sterility.

In embryos, all cell types are rapidly dividing and many signals must pass between cells to direct the morphologic development as well as the differentiation of immature cells so they can perform the functions characteristic of postembryonic life. For this reason x-ray technicians always ask a woman if there is any chance she is pregnant before they expose her. If she answers affirmatively, the technician will protect her pelvic cavity from radiation with a lead apron.

Hypothetical Gigantism by Mutation in Ants

The induction of gigantism in ants as depicted in the film *Them!* would presumably occur by means of a radiation-induced developmental mutation. In this case the mutation would have occurred in a gene that programs the extent of cell division that occurs during development. For example, human gigantism can be caused by the oversecretion of human growth hormone by the pituitary gland. This overproduction alters childhood development, particularly of bones, to spur growth to heights of seven and eight feet. After childhood such overproduction of growth hormone produces a condition called acromegaly, in which bones of the hands, feet, and face enlarge somewhat but no increase in height occurs. Despite the identification of these abnormally tall people as giants, the gigantism does not even double the size of the individual.

The giant ants of the film are closer to 150 times normal size than to the factor of perhaps a maximum of 1.5 occurring in humans. These giant ants are so large that they would be biological impossibilities without major modifications in their anatomy and biochemistry. The cells of insects, like the cells of humans, require oxygen for their survival. However, ants do not have lungs for gas exchange; instead they have branching systems of tubes called tracheae that lead from their body surfaces deep into the interior of their bodies. At the body surface oxygen enters the tubes via openings called spiracles and diffuses inward, where it eventually reaches the individual body cells. This distribution system depends on simple diffusion of the oxygen rather than the active movement of air in the bellows-like fashion in which human lungs perform. Physiologists calculate that ants as large as those in the movie could not function like their smaller, normal-sized counterparts. The diffusion time of oxygen through the ants' tracheae changes with the square of the distance to be covered. Thus, an ant about an inch long will have diffusion times that are 10,000 times shorter than an ant that is 100 inches long. A giant ant's oxygen exchange would be so slow that the ant would be very lethargic at best and at worst would suffocate. This assumes that the anatomy of giant ants is similar to that of smaller, ordinary ants. There is suggestive evidence that insects have not easily evolved different anatomies for oxygen exchange in that the fossil records shows insects always to have been much smaller than the ants depicted in *Them!* Perhaps the largest insects that ever existed were the so-called giant dragonflies that lived during the era of the dinosaurs. These giant dragonflies had wingspans of about 30 inches. Since body length in dragonflies is about half of the wingspan, these insects must have had bodies in the range of 12–15 inches, much smaller than the 10-foot-long giant ants in the film.

Another obstacle to gigantism in insects relates to their having an exoskeleton, which is shed in a molting process as they grow. Anatomists have calculated that the relatively diminutive bodies of insects are perfectly suited to the molting process, for the insects' bodies are so light that they can withstand brief periods without the support of a skeletal framework. Larger bodies would collapse under their own weight, be unable to function normally, and be subject to injury or attack during molting periods. It is also uncertain whether the material of the exoskeleton, a polysaccharide called chitin, would be able to support the weight of a massive giant ant. In addition to ants, other living things that utilize chitin in their support structures are quite small (such as other arthropods, including crabs, lobsters, and shrimp, and fungi, which use chitin in their cell walls).

Another genetic change that might cause an increase in body size is polyploidy, a condition in which cells contain multiples of the usual genetic information. A normal diploid body cell with a set of paired chromosomes is called 2N. If there are three of each chromosome type instead of two, the cell is triploid, or 3N. The bananas purchased at grocery stores are usually triploid. Normal diploid bananas are only 3–4 inches long. A drawback to this mechanism for the ants is that polyploidy is tolerated in plants but not in animals. The apparatus of cell division does not accommodate extra sets of chromosomes in animals.

SCIENTIFIC COMMENTARY

Biology.   The footprint of the ant is probably accurate if the ant is simply a larger version of a desert ant. It appears to be a representation of the arolium, the adhesive pad of the foot.

Some ants vibrate body parts to produce sounds that typically are not in the range of human hearing. Stridulation, as the activity is called, is similar to sound production by crickets. Its purpose is unknown, but giant ants might produce lower frequencies, which would then be audible to human beings. The pulling out of the walls of the trailer and the store must have been performed by the mandibles of the giant ants.

Many ants do use formic acid to kill their prey. Some spray formic acid from openings on each side of the sting, and the sting admits acid into the wound; others have no sting and open wounds with their mandibles. Formic acid is quite caustic, and it will raise blisters that last 10 days on human skin. Like any acid, it will promote painful sensations. Some ants can spray formic acid 25–50 centimeters. Dr. Medford says that the giant ants belong to the species *Camponotus vicinus* Mayr. It belongs to the subfamily Formicinae, which defend themselves by spraying venom alone or combining biting with venom spraying; they are not a stinging group. *Camponotus* species are wood ants, which nest in rotten wood and perhaps also under stones. The carpenter ants that sometimes invade human homes belong to this genus. *Camponotus* seems an unlikely genus for the giant ants, since they are shown living in the open desert areas and possessing stings.

• Dr. Medford says to shoot the ant's antennae because the ant will be "helpless" without them. Ants survive very well with their antennae removed; some become very peaceful, others very aggressive. The antennae do contain sense organs, and the overall behavior of ants whose antennae are removed is distorted at the least.

Radiation Biology, Genetics.   The existence of the giant ant is attributed to mutations caused by radiation from the first atomic bomb explosion at White Sands, New Mexico. The subject of mutations is treated in the "Scientific Principles" section.

It is questionable whether mutations caused in ants nine years earlier would take so long to be recognized. That a queen ant can found a nest, lay eggs, and have them develop into worker ants in a period of time on the order of one month suggests that the giant ants would have appeared very soon after the atomic blast. Since a queen ant typically lays tens of thousands of eggs per month and the worker ants resulting from these eggs live five years or so, all of New Mexico would have been overrun within a year after the atomic bomb explosion. Perhaps the small actual number reflects the paucity of food in the desert for giant ants, but if that were the case it seems strange the ants had not previously harmed humans or their habitations.

Another possible source of mutation that is raised by Dr. Medford is lingering radiation. In this case, surely organisms besides the ants would have been affected. The desert locale does not appear to be so isolated that mutated organisms would go unnoticed. Thus the lingering radiation idea seems unlikely.

Dr. Medford may view lingering radiation as providing for a succession of mutations that would provide the alterations necessary to produce a giant ant. If lingering radiation produced a succession of mutations, some of the intermediate forms should have been found. There is no evidence at all for successive mutations in the film. Mathematically, sequential mutations are improbable. For example, suppose that there exists a very high probability of 1 in 1,000 for a first mutation by the radiation, 1 in 1,000 for a second mutation, and 1 in 1,000 for a third mutation required to get to the giant ant forms. All mutations must occur in the same individual, and that probability is $0.001 \times 0.001 \times 0.001$, or 10^{-9}, a one in a billion chance of such a combination. Then, if the mutation is recessive, it would take interbreeding of heterozygous populations to form homozygous ants that express the mutation in their phenotype. It is also likely that the radiation levels would drop off with time and further reduce the probability of successful, successive mutations.

Chemistry, Biology. Bazookas are used to deliver and ignite phosphorus around the entrance of the ants' nest so they will stay inside it. During World War II phosphorus was used as an incendiary, so it is quite plausible that these weapons would have been available for use against the ants.

It is not clear whether the cyanide gas would quickly kill the ants throughout the giant nest. First, cyanide gas, which is 6% lighter than air, would diffuse slowly in air and penetrate the nest poorly. Second, some ants are reported to resist drowning and to survive for up to a day when their nest territory is flooded. Also, some ants are reported to be quite

resistant to cyanide. If the giant ants had similar resistance, they probably would have been unaffected by the cyanide gas after such a brief, spotty exposure. Further, the limited resistance to cyanide and flooding suggests a likely mechanism to allow for longer airways and diffusion times and thus support respiration in giants. It is a capacity to conduct anaerobic metabolism that produces the limited resistance to cyanide and flooding, and the enhancement of that characteristic would give mutants a reduced need for oxygen.

Biology. The interior of the ant nest is fairly accurately depicted. There is a great deal of variation among species in layout and building materials. Since the real species is in question, the nest architecture cannot be discussed with any precision.

It is true that desert ants make nests that are deep relative to their body size; however, the giant ants would be constrained from duplicating this nest feature because a desert soil layer is likely to be too shallow.

• The Medfords discover that the giant ants hatch directly from eggs without larval or pupal stages occurring before adulthood. This implausible modification of development avoids the problem of providing support to giant bodies after a molt before the new exoskeleton hardens. However, it is difficult to envision such a change except as requiring multiple mutations in development.

• Ants do fly, and they do make organized war and take slaves. Although few species are exclusively carnivorous or even prefer a carnivorous diet, ants can be carnivorous; army ants in some parts of the world move in a column that may be miles in length, devouring everything in their paths. An ant can lift up to 20 times its weight.

• The number of ants depicted in the nest in Los Angeles may be too small. A queen ant can lay tens of thousands of eggs per month. The drunk reported seeing giant ants for a long time, and he had been a patient over a 5-month period. In that time there could have been thousands of worker ants to defend the nest; each ant would have fought to the death against the army. A possible explanation is that the mutations that created the giant ants also resulted in high egg mortality. Another factor might be that the ants had difficulty in finding enough food and ate eggs. Queens who do not forage eat many eggs before a few hatch to supply food for all. Some queens do forage, a practice that increases the size of the first brood, but many species' queens do not leave the queen's chamber or claustral cell. These initially live on resorbed wing muscle and eggs.

CLASSROOM ACTIVITIES

Exercises to Extend Learning

1. What happened to the trailer in the desert? Why was the money still in the trailer? Why were sugar cubes found scattered?

2. What connection is there between the ants and the formic acid found in the storekeeper's body?

3. Do ants die when their antennae are removed?

4. The giant ants are called mutants by the scientists. What is a mutant? What is a mutation? Can radiation cause mutations? Can an atomic bomb cause mutations?

5. Do you think the exoskeleton of an ant could support a giant ant? Why or why not? How does an ordinary ant take in air to get its oxygen? Could the giant ants "breathe" well enough to get a supply of oxygen to their cells? In other words, could the mutants really be expected to have adequate respiratory capability?

6. What do the Medfords find very different in the development of the giant ants compared to ordinary ants? Do you think such a change in life history is possible? Why?

7. Since the Los Angeles nest was apparently several months old, why do you think there were so few giant ants? How could the giant ants have carried off 40 tons of sugar?

8. How long before the time of the story was the atomic bomb exploded at White Sands? If it caused mutants, when do you think they would have appeared?

9. List some of the behaviors and other characteristics of ants mentioned or depicted in *Them!* Which ones are accurate, and which ones are erroneous?

Topics for Further Discussion

Biology. Dr. Medford cites a biblical prophecy that the "beasts shall reign over the Earth." A colleague confirms that humanity will be wiped out by the ants in about a year if the two escaped queen ants are not destroyed. How did the colleague estimate this time period?

Sociology. Should the government have immediately announced the existence of the giant ants and asked for public cooperation in finding the two escaped queen ants?

Biology. Although ants do not go out in the desert during the hottest part of the day, elsewhere they normally forage in daylight. Is it therefore likely that only one drunk would have seen them during a several month period in Los Angeles?

• Furthermore, how could the ants carry off 40 tons of sugar? The sugar was probably stacked on skids weighing several hundred pounds each. The giant ants carried off the loaded skids. But, why didn't the guard hear them tearing open the boxcar and carrying off the skids?

Radiation.   Does the picture describe a realistic danger in the atomic age? What are the more likely dangers?

• Why do x-ray technicians stand in a different room from the patient when x-rays are taken? Why do patients wear lead aprons while x-rays are taken?

Biology.   Why do you think Dr. Medford stated that no newly hatched queens had left the nest in the storm drains?

Portrayal of Scientists.   Do you think the Drs. Medford are believable characters? Is either a stereotype?

LITERARY COMMENTARY

Them! has no specific literary source; however, it is a dramatic presentation of familiar science fiction themes derived from Darwinian evolution (as popularly conceived, and sometimes grossly misconceived) and modified by increasing scientific knowledge and practical experience. If radiation hazard and the consequent mutations is one theme, another is the perpetual contest between human beings and insects. Both of these themes, however, fit into the larger theme of humanity's rashly and unwittingly producing dangerous effects in the biosphere, primarily by means of scientific development and technological application without regard for potential long-term consequences.

Mutation, a concept inherent in Darwinian theory, occurs in *Them!* as a direct result of atomic bomb tests in the New Mexico desert, producing the giant ants. In 1930, John Taine's novel *The Iron Star* showed a mutagenic meteor transforming the local wildlife in a region in Africa into exotic shapes and sizes that were hazardous to man. Similarly, Alfred Gordon Bennett's *The Demigods*, published in 1939, focused specifically on the mutation of ants into a giant form, although without the intervention of nuclear tests to explain the mutation. More recently, Keith Roberts, a British novelist, showed giant wasps resulting from the radiation of a nuclear test in his 1966 novel, *The Furies*.

As practical knowledge of radiation effects increased, stories of human mutation became more common. One of the earliest novels dealing with this theme was John Taine's *Seeds of Life* (1931; reprinted 1951), in which an irradiated man becomes a superman but fails to realize the damage he has done to the genes he passes to the next generation. After the explosion of the atomic bomb in 1945, stories about human mutation because of exposure to radiation became frequent. Between 1948 and 1950, for example, Wilmar H. Shiras published a series of stories, beginning with "In Hiding," that describe the discovery of brilliant children, vastly more intelligent and creative than normal. Their parents had been exposed to radiation while working on the development of the atomic bomb. The stories were published as a novel, *Children of the Atom*, in 1953. Using the same "superchild" theme, Jerome Bixby's 1953 story, "It's a *Good* Life," demonstrates what terror such a child could cause a normal community if it could enforce the gratification of its every whim.

More realistically, post–atomic war stories such as Lester del Rey's *The Eleventh Commandment* (1962; revised 1970) deal with the lethal effects of radiation-induced mutation. In this novel, the gene pool of the survivors is so damaged, and the mutation rate is so swift, with such disastrous results, that the postwar church encourages limitless reproduction in an attempt to produce a stable, human-normal, reproductive population. Roger Zelazny's *Damnation Alley* and Harlan Ellison's "A Boy and His Dog," both published in 1969, also portray post-holocaust worlds of human and animal mutations, expressing concern about the defective genes caused by the radiation or about the necessity of establishing an adequate gene pool among small groups of survivors. Both have been adapted into movies.

More recently, "mutation" novels have dealt with the hazards of pollution and of biochemical warfare. In 1966 Frank Herbert published *The Green Brain*. This novel shows humans determined to control all insect life with insecticides, creating a "green zone" clear of pests, with the surviving insects gathering in the "red zone" in South America. There the surviving insects, mutated by the insecticides, achieve a corporate intelligence. A group of these insects cling together in an imitation of the human form, sneak into the "green zone," and the war is on. Alan Scott's 1971 novel, *The Anthrax Mutation*, supposes that a biological warfare laboratory has created an especially lethal form of anthrax. Through a laboratory accident, the mutated anthrax escapes to infest common bats, which then put the entire world at hazard.

Them! started a rash of imitative films during the 1950s, but it remains the best of the "radiation-induced monster mutation" films. Some of its lesser imitations are *Tarantula* (1955) and *It Came from*

Beneath the Sea, also released in 1955, in which a giant octopus mutated by radiation terrorizes the California coast. *Them!* is still by far the better and more credible film.

CHAPTER BIBLIOGRAPHY

Film References

Warren, Bill. *"Them!" Keep Watching the Skies! American Science Fiction Movies of the Fifties: Volume One, 1950-1957*. Jefferson, NC: McFarland, 1982, pp. 188-95.

Film Reviews

America 91, 3 July 1954: 367.
Catholic World 179 (May 1954): 144.
Commonweal 60, 18 June 1954: 269.
Farm Journal 78 (June 1954): 141.
National Parent Teacher 48 (June 1954): 40.
New Yorker 30, 26 June 1954: 61.
Newsweek 43, 7 June 1954: 56.
Saturday Review 37, 5 June 1954: 27.
Scholastic 64, 12 May 1954: 29.
Time 62, 19 Oct. 1953: 112.
Time 64, 19 July 1954: 79.

CHAPTER 7

The Andromeda Strain

- Universal Pictures (USA), 1970, color, wide screen, 130 minutes
- **Credits:** *Producer and director*, Robert Wise; *screenplay*, Nelson Gidding, based on the novel by Michael Crichton; *cinematographer*, Richard Kline; *special effects*, Douglas Trumbull; *music*, Gil Melle
- **Cast:** Arthur Hill (Jeremy Stone), James Olson (Mark Hall), David Wayne (Charles Dutton), Kate Reid (Ruth Leavitt), and Paula Kelly (Karen Anson)
- **Distributors:** *16 mm* — Swank Motion Pictures, Inc., 350 Vanderbilt Motor Parkway, Hauppauge, NY 11787, (800) 645-7501; *Videotape* — MCA Videocassette Inc., 70 Universal City Plaza, Universal City, CA 91608

PLOT SUMMARY

The film opens with a statement that we are about to see an accurate account of an actual four-day crisis. The government is shortly to release the details of this crisis, which involved Wildfire and Project Scoop.

First Day

It is February 5, 1971, at Piedmont, New Mexico (population 68). Two airmen enter the town to recover a satellite that has fallen to Earth. They are locating it using a homing device inside the satellite. Concern increases when they report that they see many dead bodies in the town. Then they see something white coming at them; a scream is heard and nothing more.

The military sends a reconnaissance plane to photograph the town. When the film it takes is reviewed, a Wildfire alert is called. This involves calling to action four civilian scientists, Jeremy Stone (a Nobel prize winner and the head of the Wildfire team), Charles Dutton, Ruth Leavitt, and Mark Hall (a physician who had considered Stone's Wildfire memoranda to be science fiction). We see that the purpose of Project Scoop is to collect extraterrestrial organisms and to evaluate their potential danger to humanity.

Second Day

There is a security meeting in Washington, D.C., at which we learn that Dr. Stone apparently did not know that Project Scoop existed. Under the Wildfire program, approximately $90 million had been spent building a more advanced receiving laboratory, equipped with a nuclear self-destruct weapon, for studying extraterrestrial organisms that might threaten Earth. In order to secure funding, Dr. Stone had told congressional leaders that the existing facilities were inadequate.

Drs. Stone and Hall begin their Wildfire work as they fly to Piedmont and drop poison gas cannisters to kill any birds who may have eaten flesh and, therefore, become contaminated. Then, dressed in protective airtight suits with self-contained oxygen supplies, they enter Piedmont. They find that all of the inhabitants of Piedmont are dead except a small baby and a drunk, who is dressed in white. They recover the satellite, which had been carried to the town physician's office and there opened, apparently releasing deadly organisms. Different victims apparently died at different rates after exposure. Some first went insane, while others died almost instantly. The blood in the victims had changed to powder. A helicopter then lifts Stone and Hall from the town, along with the satellite, the baby, and the drunk.

Dr. Stone requests that a nuclear bomb be dropped immediately on Piedmont to "neutralize" the extraterrestrial organism.

Drs. Dutton and Leavitt arrive at the Wildfire research facility. It is built underground beneath an agricultural station, as its existence is top secret.

The research team meets together; they are reminded that the facility has five levels, each level biologically cleaner than the level above. It will take them 16 hours to go through the decontamination procedures in order to reach the fifth level. At the bottom of the facility is a nuclear bomb that will be activated automatically if there is an accident that threatens to release the extraterrestrial organisms into the atmosphere. Once the bomb is activated, there are five minutes in which to stop it from exploding. The only key to deactivate the bomb is given to Dr. Hall because he is male and single; therefore, he is entrusted with the decision under the "odd-man hypothesis."

Third Day

The research team is on the fourth level. Dr. Stone summarizes their goals:

1. Detect the organism if it is still present in the satellite.
2. Characterize the organism.
3. Control the organism — how can it be neutralized or destroyed?

The research team then proceeds to level five and begins to work. They expose first a rat and then a rhesus monkey to the satellite; both die immediately. Then they determine how the organism spreads in a victim. They find that the organism enters the body through the lungs and causes the blood to coagulate, beginning in the lungs and then spreading throughout the body. The organism is spread through the air, and by using different-sized filters they determine that its size is between one and two microns, large enough to be a cell.

They then examine the satellite capsule and find a tiny speck inside it. The speck turns out to be a piece of stone-like material covered by green spots that change in size as they watch. These are the extraterrestrial organism, which seems to grow when exposed to light.

The Andromeda Strain: A highly trained nurse/technician wearing an isolation suit in the Wildfire infirmary. (Photo: Museum of Modern Art/Film Stills Archive. Courtesy of Universal Pictures.)

Hall attempts to understand the reason that the drunk and the baby survived. He notes that the drunk has an ulcer and "treats" it with aspirin and alcohol, while the baby cries much of the time. But Hall can't determine what is similar in the physiology of both survivors.

Meanwhile, the president has not authorized the dropping of a nuclear bomb on Piedmont. An accident, possibly related to the introduction of the alien organism, occurs. An airplane flying at 23,000 feet crashes 60 miles away from Piedmont after the disintegration of all its rubber-like components. When the crash site is investigated, all that remains of the pilot are his bones. Meanwhile, the Wildfire facility is unaware of these developments because of a mechanical fault in its incoming message-receiving unit.

By this time the team concludes from the satellite's construction that the Project Scoop satellite was apparently searching for the ultimate biological weapon — an extraterrestrial organism! They analyze both the stone-like material and the green spots. The material is actually plastic-like in character and contains hydrogen, oxygen, carbon, sulfur, silicon, and other elements. The green organism contains no amino acids or nucleic acids and has evolved in a totally different way from earthly organisms. They attempt to characterize and understand the organism's physiology in hopes of learning the key to controlling it. Dr. Leavitt has an epileptic seizure while screening the results of the growth tests and blanks out when the computer indicates no growth on one medium; she erroneously reports that the alien organism grows on all media tested.

Fourth Day

The research team obtains a code designation for the alien organism — the Andromeda strain. They examine the organism under the electron microscope. It looks like a crystal and divides in the vacuum while being bombarded with the electron beam. They assert that "Andromeda" absorbs energy like a nuclear reactor and changes energy directly into matter with no excretion. It is composed of identical molecules. While they are observing it, it both grows and alters its structure.

An accident exposes Dutton to the organism, but he lives because it has now "mutated" into a nonlethal form. Dr. Hall observes Leavitt having an epileptic seizure and, fearing that she overlooked something because of her epilepsy, gets the computer to recheck the data and finds that the Andromeda strain originally could only grow in a narrow range of pH, namely between 7.39 and 7.43.

At this point, a mutant of the Andromeda strain starts to dissolve the gaskets around the isolation chamber, and the protective nuclear device is triggered to explode in five minutes. Dr. Hall manages to disarm it in the nick of time. Earlier, Dr. Stone had rescinded his prior request to drop a nuclear bomb on Piedmont. The scientists now believe that a nuclear explosion would simply feed large amounts of energy into the organisms and cause many mutations.

As the film ends, the main colony of the Andromeda strain has moved off the California coast. It is expected to be neutralized by the ocean, which has a higher pH than the human body and thus does not support the life of Andromeda.

At a congressional hearing, Dr. Stone is asked what to do if another extraterrestrial organism reaches the Earth. He has no reassuring answer to give.

Special Effects.   They are minimal. The laboratory instrumentation is impressive looking. The lighting effects are excellent.

SCIENTIFIC PRINCIPLES RELATED TO THE FILM

The Origin of Life

The idea that earthly life has been affected in the past and may be affected again by life beyond Earth is a recurring one in both science fiction and scientific circles. The study of life outside of Earth's atmosphere is called exobiology. It encompasses study by astronomers of the composition of interstellar space and astronomical bodies; by chemists, biologists, and geologists of how life probably arose on Earth; and by microbiologists and chemists of extraterrestrial samples and of space vehicles. While no direct evidence so far exists for life elsewhere, some characteristics of the galaxy compared to earthly life forms suggest that life might exist outside the biosphere.

The realm beyond Earth's atmosphere, space used to be considered a frigid vacuum devoid of molecules; however, recent findings by microwave spectroscopy have revealed small molecules in space. Hydrocyanic acid (HCN), carbon monoxide (CO), methane (CH_4), ammonia (NH_3), methanol (CH_3OH), formic acid ($HCOOH$), formaldehyde (CH_2O), thioformaldehyde (H_2CS), acetaldehyde (CH_3CHO), formamide ($HCONH_2$), water (H_2O), and numerous other small molecules have been detected. According to enthusiasts of exobiology, since such supra-atomic forms of biologically abundant elements exist in space, then perhaps they could interact in a way that produces life forms.

Prebiotic evolution, in order to supply the biochemicals for life, must reach a stage beyond the existence of atoms and simple molecules

and provide both simple bioorganic molecules and macromolecules. One
argument in favor of the possibility of such a progression is that there is a
good supply of raw materials, namely, carbon, hydrogen, oxygen, nitrogen, sulfur, and phosphorus (Table 7.1). These bioelements are among the
most abundant in the universe. In fact, simple bioorganic molecules have
been found on meteorites and in lunar rock samples. Acid hydrolysis of
lunar rock yields common amino acids with glycine, alanine, and glutamic
acid the most abundant. Careful analysis of the possibility for contamination by humans or rocket exhaust has eliminated that option for many;
others believe the similarity of these lunar findings to those in meteorites
(which are never obtained in pristine form) mitigates the results.

Only on Earth does the progression to greater complexity seem to
have continued beyond that found in space or on various celestial solid
bodies. Various laboratory methods have simulated some of the steps that
probably occurred to generate macromolecules from simple bioorganic
molecules. Reducing agents such as hypophosphorous acid at elevated
temperatures on the order of 170°C polymerize amino acids to form
proteinoids, which possess many of the critical properties to proceed to
the formation of cells. Proteinoids display various enzyme-like activities
and readily associate into larger assemblages, such as those called microspheres and nucleoproteinoid particles, which are in turn suggestive of
the ability to form proto-cell membranes and protochromatin, respectively. Models of primitive proto-cells, such as coacervate droplets made of
oppositely charged colloids and including enzyme molecules, indicate

TABLE 7.1.   Abundance of Elements

| Element | Gram atoms per gram atom of carbon | |
	Universe	Earth's crust
Hydrogen	1.1×10^4	52
Helium	8.9×10^3	2.8×10^{-5}
Oxygen	6.0	1.1×10^3
Neon	2.5	$>1 \times 10^{-6}$
Nitrogen	1.9	0.12
Carbon	(1.0)	(1.0)
Silicon	0.29	3.7×10^2
Magnesium	0.26	32
Iron	0.17	41
Sulfur	0.11	0.59

their ability to support the internal actions of enzymes. For example, synthesis of starch and of polynucleotides has been detected in them.

Lipids, responsible for key properties of membranes, tend to aggregate into liposomes in water-rich conditions. These small structures form barriers that establish compartments, just as the membranes of cells do. Membranes are also rich in protein, and it is interesting that microspheres tend to pick up lipids, thus bringing together these major membrane components.

The research conducted so far supports the idea that cells could have arisen on the primitive Earth. There is no need to suppose that life began elsewhere in the universe and seeded the Earth some time in the past (and possibly in the present, also).

Virology

Just how small an entity may qualify as living is a related consideration, for if lifeless molecules somehow become associated either terrestrially or extraterrestrially to form living things, the transition from non-living to living must occur. It is tempting to state that life is associated only with single cells or assemblages of cells. Such clear boundaries may not be established unequivocally, and the problems arise due to the existence of the two simplest earthly organisms, viruses and viroids. Neither is free-living and capable of reproducing itself without interacting with living cells. Viruses, which are probably the inspiration for the Andromeda strain, are composed of nucleic acid, either DNA or RNA, in a core and a protein coat, or capsid. The protein coat molecules are regularly and often symmetrically arranged around the nucleic acid. Their small size and small number of component molecules give viruses the unusual property of being crystallizable. Crystalline arrays of virus particles sometimes can be seen inside infected cells. Viroids are simpler than viruses and consist only of naked RNA. Recently a third type of noncellular infectious agent has been claimed — the prion, similar to a viroid but made of protein only.

Both viruses and viroids were first noticed and discovered because of their pathology; one of the most famous and well-understood viruses causes a disease in tobacco and is named tobacco mosaic virus (TMV). Each virus particle is cylindrical in shape, with a regular array of protein coat molecules surrounding the RNA core. Numerous other viruses are known to infect humans and cause a wide array of diseases, such as AIDS, chicken pox, shingles, common colds, encephalitis, Parkinson's disease, and pneumonia. Viruses are suspected of playing a role in many other diseases, including some cancers, multiple sclerosis, arthritis, and juvenile diabetes.

Viruses can reproduce only upon entering a living cell, taking over its internal "machinery," and producing new components of the virus that self-assemble into new infective particles or virions, as illustrated in Figure 7.1. The virus's nucleic acid provides essential genetic information for the process, but some host genes may be used. The protein of the virus in some cases has enzymatic activity inside the host cell.

One cannot call viruses nonliving because they have a key characteristic of life, namely, the ability to reproduce. As with cellular organisms, the viability of a virus can be destroyed by various chemical or physical means. Viruses are certainly on the fringes of life and demonstrate a continuum from nonliving to living things.

SCIENTIFIC COMMENTARY

Immunology.   In Piedmont we are shown a dead dog and a dead cat, presumably victims of the unearthly pestilence. If the disease is not infectious only to humans, probably there is a good chance the birds would have succumbed also.

Physiology.   The discovery that the blood of all victims has turned to powder is implausible. Blood is mainly water. Where did all the water go?

Exobiology.   The suits worn by Drs. Stone and Hall when they enter the town are apparently decontaminated by being subjected to some form of radiation. However, the Andromeda strain absorbs radiation. Thus when they remove the suits, the organism would have killed them unless it had already mutated to a nonlethal form. Since the samples brought from Piedmont remain lethal in later lab tests, they were lucky to survive getting out of their suits.

Microbiology.   The elaborate decontamination of the research team seems foolish. First of all, it is impossible to decontaminate living human beings. They will continue to harbor and release microorganisms. For example, it is illogical to protect the face and hair during the xenon lamp decontamination. Second, if the research facility was as good as was claimed, it would isolate the researchers from the Andromeda strain completely. Even routine microbiological techniques yield uncontaminated cultures. Third, the capsule was opened in the Piedmont physician's

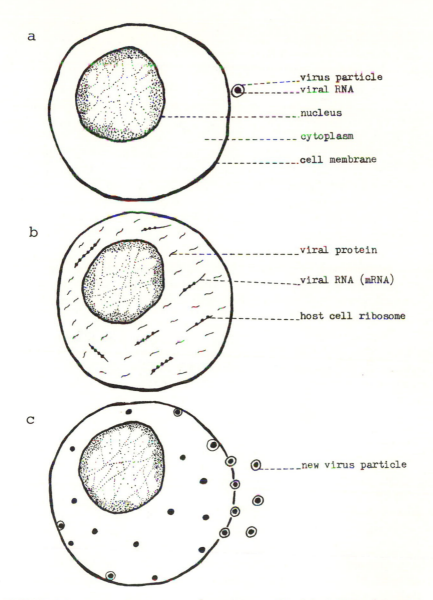

FIGURE 7.1. (a) An RNA virus approaches a cell to inject its nucleic acid (and an enzyme to make more nucleic acid) into the cell; (b) The cell makes many copies of the viral RNA, which then serves as messenger RNA (mRNA) to synthesize viral protein with the aid of the host cell's ribosomes; (c) Viral RNA and protein associate to form new virions (virus particles), which are released from the host cell, usually killing it in the process.

office and was itself contaminated, a problem that should have posed greater problems for the scientific studies than microbes on the researchers' bodies.

Exobiology. The statement that Rudolph Karp had discovered bacteria in meteorites is nonsense. No living organisms have been found in meteorites or on the surface of Mars or on the Moon or any other place besides Earth.

• Dutton claims that the Andromeda strain might be an intelligent microorganism. However, intelligence requires the ability to acquire, process, and transmit complex information, and this would require molecular information handling, which is unknown. Some computer research and development effort (artificial intelligence) is aimed at achieving just this goal.

Microbiology. Determining the size of Andromeda by using a series of increasingly larger holes in air filters seems like a perfectly logical solution to the problem and is in use at present for similar purposes.

Diagnostic Medicine. We learn that Dutton will do an isotope study on a monkey and then see a device called a Magna scanner. The process appears to be related to that of the newly introduced NMR scanners, but there is no clear explanation of the basis for the patterns shown on the monitor to represent the spread of the organism through the monkey's body.

Optics. During the repetitive scans of the satellite capsule, the microscope was too far away from the part of the capsule being viewed, and the relative magnifications were not in proportion to the pictures that are shown. For example, going from a $60\times$ to an $80\times$ lens, the picture should represent an increase of $1/3$ in the magnification; however, the picture we see appears to be several times larger.

Mechanics. It is claimed that the piece of stone-like material embedded in the capsule is too small to have made that indentation but that perhaps it had different properties in space. The depth of the indentation reflects the mass and velocity of the impacting object. The mass of the object is identical in space or on Earth.

Engineering. The inside of the satellite capsule is covered with a mesh. Clearly in outer space the top of the capsule opens in order to attempt to catch a small meteorite within the capsule. If the meteorite penetrated the mesh, it would likely be stopped by the metal sides of the capsule below and the mesh would prevent fragments from flying out; that is, it was a scoop for meteorites.

Microbial Physiology.   We see the green spots growing under the optical microscope. Ostensibly the organism is absorbing light used to illuminate the object and converting that energy directly into mass. No known organism can do that. Only photosynthetic organisms can convert electromagnetic radiation into biomass when they fix carbon, but even this process is not direct.

Biochemistry and Genetics.   The first clear evidence that the organism has mutated is the disintegration of the plane's plastic substances and the flesh of the pilot's body. Presumably the carbon compounds were another source of nutrients for the organism. This suggests that the reason other humans in the surrounding area did not die with the same symptoms as those in Piedmont is that the entire colony at Piedmont must have mutated. It is highly unlikely that an extremely virulent organism would mutate into exclusively nonvirulent organisms. Therefore, the Air Force personnel investigating at the crash site should not have remained healthy and alive.

Physical Chemistry.   A mass spectrometer is used in the film to determine the elementary composition of the black speck and the green spots. A mass spectrometer is normally employed not to determine the elementary composition of a sample but instead to promote fragmentation of a molecule and then use the sizes of the fragments as clues to the structure of the sample. When the molecular weight and structural formula are known, the elementary composition can be calculated if desired.

Molecular Biology.   The elementary analysis reveals that Andromeda contains only hydrogen, carbon, nitrogen, and oxygen. Furthermore, it contains neither amino acids nor nucleic acids. The team agrees that it represents a totally different kind of evolution from Earth's. Should such an organism exist, that conclusion would be accurate, since the simplest reproducing entities known are RNA viroids and prions (proposed but not firmly established), which are themselves, respectively, nucleic acids with an elementary composition of carbon, hydrogen, oxygen, nitrogen, and phosphorous and proteins with the elementary composition of carbon, hydrogen, oxygen, nitrogen, and sulfur. Viroids and prions, like Andromeda, are infectious, but they cause long-lasting, chronic diseases such as scrapie and kuru, not fast-moving, rapidly fatal diseases as Andromeda did.

Microbiology.   We are shown scores of petri dishes used to test various growth media. It seems implausible that the tiny green specks could have provided sufficient inoculum for so many plates. In addition, we see only one plate register for no growth, yet Hall later learns from the computer the pH-dependent growth curve for the Andromeda strain. This seems strange, since a set of plates to test pH-dependence was likely to have been set up and screened along with the other growth tests. A number of them would have had to show no growth.

Another problem of the growth studies is that we have no mention of purification of the organism. The space capsule was open to the environment in the Piedmont physician's office and should have carried earthly microbes with it, which in turn would have been contaminants growing on plates with Andromeda. The assay for growth appeared to be a photometric one, which probably would not distinguish between growth of ordinary bacteria and Andromeda. Did Andromeda consume microbes that fell upon it and stay pure?

Communications.   The numerous communication problems that occur in the film are implausible. There surely would have been multiple links to the Wildfire facility.

Electron Microscopy.   Cutting a stub containing a fixed specimen embedded in a hard polymeric resin is shown accurately. The instrument, an ultramicrotome, advances the stub automatically to be cut by a glass or diamond knife. The thin slice (about $1/10$ of a micron thick) is then placed on a small copper grid, which is placed in a cassette that goes into the electron microscope. The specimen is studied by using an electron beam in place of light for revealing organizational patterns in the specimen. The electrons pass through specimen components to different degrees; it is the variations in transmission of the electron beam that provides a pattern of the specimen's structure. The microscopist sees the specimen ordinarily on a TV-like screen and can photograph the image also.

In reality the team would have had difficulty in processing the specimen so quickly, since the specimen must be fixed, dehydrated, and infiltrated with resin, and the stub must be cured so it will be hard enough to cut very thin slices from it. Earthly specimens are killed by the processing and would show no activity of any kind while being examined. Electron microscopes' vacuum pumps are just as noisy when they pump down as the one in the film.

Molecular Biology.   Leavitt speculates that Andromeda, crystalline in form, consisting of only one type of molecule and growing before their eyes while in the electron microscope, is using wedge-shaped areas to form compartments for biochemical functions. Such a statement is not applicable to earthly life forms, which ordinarily are inactive when they are in highly ordered, relatively anhydrous states. Indeed, our concept of biochemistry is based largely on interactions between different molecules in a watery environment.

Physics.   The idea that Andromeda is a little nuclear reactor is incorrect. A reactor breaks apart heavy atomic nuclei of elements, such as uranium, into smaller nuclei (waste products). Andromeda seems to function in reverse of a reactor, taking in energy and producing matter, not starting with matter and giving off energy. Furthermore, the claim that a nuclear bomb exploding at the base of the facility would create countless new mutations in Andromeda is nonsense. A hydrogen bomb, for example, would produce a fireball at its center in which the temperature would be millions of degrees. At that elevated temperature, all of the atoms would be torn apart. Therefore, the Andromeda strain would no longer exist. However, it may be that a nuclear bomb dropped on Piedmont might not destroy all of the Andromeda strain if some of the organisms were outside of the fireball. Those indeed might be able to absorb energy and mutate.

Computerized Microbiology.   A computer simulation is performed, using computerized data on Andromeda, and while the team views it, they see nonuniformity in the growth pattern, which they interpret as mutation. This capability is far-fetched at best.

Medicine.   During the first days of the crisis, we see Leavitt occasionally having minor seizures. She seems to freeze, cease conscious functioning for a few minutes, and then have no memory of the seizure except as she discovers that she has "lost" time. Finally, on the fourth day, she has a seizure with convulsions. The depictions of the seizures are very accurate. It does seem strange that the medical support staff do not recognize epilepsy but instead fear she has caught "the germ."

Microbial Physiology and Human Physiology.   Hall concludes and Stone concurs that the computer-generated curve for pH dependence of Andromeda's growth provides the solution to saving humanity from Andromeda. The growth curve is bell-shaped and shows no growth below 7.39 and above 7.43. This property seems highly unlikely, both because an organism from space, a very low-water environment, is unlikely to

depend on pH at all and because the range given is far too narrow to be
believable if the growth is actually pH-dependent.

Also, the old man, Jackson, and the baby are supposed to have
survived because their blood pH's are abnormal. Jackson's pH is shown
as 7.31, a pH that is definitely acidemic. The baby's pH is shown as 7.43
and labeled alkalemia, an incorrect designation. The normal pH of blood
is nominally 7.40, but most clinicians consider the entire range from
7.35–7.45 normal. Body cells tolerate acidemia only to about 7.1 before
death results. It is more difficult to generate long-lasting alkalemia, since
body cells constantly generate CO_2 as they metabolize carbon compounds
for energy. In the watery environment of the body, the CO_2, often called
the respiratory acid, is in equilibrium with carbonic acid as follows:

$$CO_2 + H_2O \rightleftharpoons H_2CO_3 \rightleftharpoons H^+ + HCO_3^+$$

Note that as CO_2 is produced, H^+ concentrations increase and the
pH decreases. The baby, with his crying, is blowing off CO_2 and raising
his pH somewhat, supposedly creating a respiratory alkalemia. It would
be hard to do this in practice for very long, and, as noted previously, the
pH given for the baby is actually a normal one. Jackson is presumably in
acidosis because the metabolism of alcohol is creating ketone bodies and
increased acidity. The same result occurs in a diabetic (or a dieter) who
metabolizes fats instead of glucose. It is not clear why Jackson should
remain acidotic for long after stopping his intake of "squeeze." The
squeeze is cited for containing ethanol and methanol by the medical
computer, but no amounts are given. Methanol, with an odd number
of carbon atoms, is toxic, and at high doses causes blindness or even
death.

Microbial Genetics.   Andromeda's facility for mutation is evident a
third time when the polychron gaskets at the Wildfire lab start to degenerate. Apparently the same type of mutant was responsible for the Air
Force pilot's crash near Piedmont. It is not clear why that instance was
accompanied by destruction of flesh and the Wildfire incident is not.

Laboratory Safety.   It is astonishing that the Wildfire installation
was designed, built, and operating with a mechanism that could isolate
Hall from access to a substation for stopping a nuclear explosion from
destroying the lab.

Meteorology and Microbiology.   At the end of the story, the airborne
Andromeda is supposed to be moving out to sea, and cloud-seeding will

then wash it into the ocean, whose pH is about 7.6–7.8. There are three problems to this "solution." The prevailing winds around California blow from the west, not the reverse as required in the film. Cloud-seeding is a very unreliable process. The growth curve provides only for a no-growth situation, which is not necessarily going to kill the organism. Among Earth's microbes, the simpler viruses are more difficult to kill than the bacteria, so Andromeda would probably be harder to kill than a virus. (Such distinctions in disinfectants' actions are made routinely by microbiologists, e.g., a *bacteriostatic* agent stops bacteria from growing, but a *bacteriocidal* agent kills them.)

CLASSROOM ACTIVITIES

Exercises to Extend Learning

1. Who or what is affected by the Andromeda strain?

2. What happens to the blood of the victims? How does this appearance of blood compare with coagulated blood you have seen? Can you think of a cause for the difference?

3. What is the purpose of the protective gear Stone and Hall wear into Piedmont? How does its design achieve that purpose?

4. Why are Stone and Hall, still wearing their protective suits, irradiated when they return to the Wildfire lab from Piedmont? Do you think this is likely to be an effective method where the Andromeda strain is involved? Why or why not?

5. Why are the Wildfire scientists undergoing the various procedures on the different levels of the facility? Can you determine whether the procedures are achieving what they are intended to? For example, does the skin actually get decontaminated by the xenon lamp treatment? If so, why should or should not the face and hair be protected? Can a human being receive all needed nutrients in an 8-ounce daily drink?

6. Describe the construction of the satellite. Why do you suppose it belonged to a project named Scoop?

7. Why does the Air Force pilot crash? What happens to him and to his equipment?

8. What was growing on the petri dishes Dr. Leavitt reviews? What were the growth tests designed to find out?

9. Why does the team want to examine their specimen in the electron microscope? How do they prepare the sample for examination?

10. How does Dr. Leavitt describe the Andromeda strain's structure? What does she think enables it to perform biochemically? Name some

common crystals that you would have at home. Do these crystals have biochemical or metabolic function such as proposed for Andromeda?

11. How do the scientists explain the ability of the Andromeda strain to use energy? Do you agree with their analogy? Why or why not? Do you think dropping an atomic bomb on Piedmont or destroying the Wildfire lab with a hydrogen bomb is likely to succeed in destroying the Andromeda strain? Why or why not?

12. What observations are made by the team when they view the computer simulation of Andromeda's appearance? Do you think a computer could really do this? Why or why not?

13. What health disorder does Dr. Leavitt have? How can you tell? Has it affected her work on the Wildfire project?

14. What does Hall find out about the pH dependence of Andromeda's growth? What is pH?

15. The normal range of pH for human body cells to operate properly is 7.35–7.45. How does this range compare to Andromeda's growth range?

16. Sea water has a pH around 7.8. What do you think will happen to Andromeda in the sea?

17. Why do the polychron gaskets of the Wildfire lab start to degenerate?

18. Why isn't Dr. Dutton killed when he is exposed to Andromeda?

Topics for Further Discussion

Psychology.   Is the odd-man hypothesis reasonable?

Public Policy.   Should the United States build a facility like Wildfire equipped with a thermonuclear self-destruct device?

Sexism.   In the book Dr. Leavitt is a man. In the film the character becomes a woman, who is portrayed as being both unpleasant personally and the weak link in the team. Is this a sexist modification?

Psychology.   Why did the technician run away when Dr. Hall asked her to help him insert the key to deactivate the nuclear bomb? Surely she must have known of the existence of the bomb and the purpose of the substation into which the key was to be inserted.

Ethics.   Do you think that Dr. Stone's comment that no first-rate institution would have taken Dr. Leavitt if her epilepsy was known is correct? If it is correct, is it appropriate and/or fair? Should Dr. Leavitt have told her Wildfire colleagues about her medical problem?

Biology.   What properties are common to all living things on Earth? Which of these properties are exhibited by Andromeda?

LITERARY COMMENTARY

The Andromeda Strain, as a novel, purports to be strictly documentary, with acknowledgments to military personnel, references to hearing reports, and citations of personnel interviews. In addition, Crichton provides a three-page bibliography of scientific articles and government documents at the end of the book. Citations of these articles and documents occur throughout the novel to create the impression of a complete and thorough account. The film conveys a pseudodocumentary style, but the effect is spoiled somewhat by the "human interest" and "dramatic" elements introduced into the film.

A major change between novel and film occurs in the principal characters, presumably to add human interest lacking in the novel and to make the characters more appealing. Stone, instead of being thin, balding, and impatient, becomes handsome and authoritarian, enforcing protocol and giving orders, a "leader" rather than a team member. Hall becomes boyishly appealing and casual, caring about his patients, rather than the irritable prima donna surgeon whose patients are merely a source of information. Charles Burton suffers a name change to Dutton, but even more he suffers a character change from a phenomenally unkempt slob to a warm and caring father figure. Patient, amusing, imaginative Peter Leavitt is transformed entirely, becoming Ruth Leavitt, crusty, uncooperative, and self-centered. Karen Anson, impersonal lab technician, undergoes a similar change, becoming sarcastic and critical of Hall's ignorance of the equipment and his treatment of patients, though nonetheless nurturant and "scared."

Apart from minor alterations, such as changing Piedmont's location from Arizona to New Mexico or using laser beams in the central core instead of ligamine darts, the major differences between novel and film seem directed toward condensing the plot to fit the visual medium, changing the date from 1967 to 1971 to gain a sense of immediacy, and focusing more on the preliminaries and persons for dramatic interest than on the actual laboratory sequences, which consume a relatively small proportion of the film. The plot abridgment's primary effect on the film is the cryptic nature of some information.

First Day

Crichton's novel indicates that Project Scoop control deliberately brought down the satellite now in Piedmont because its orbit had become unstable, probably through collision with a meteorite or some piece of orbital "junk" still in space from the hundreds of American and Russian satellites previously launched. This lends credibility to the later discovery of the abnormal nature of the "meteorite" in the capsule. Perhaps it *is* a piece of plastic. In the novel, a computer error causes a delay in collecting the four scientists of the Wildfire team, slowing the Wildfire project. In addition, each team member receives a Project Scoop file to read in transit, and they learn for the first time of the existence and purpose of Project Scoop: its function is to collect potentially harmful extraterrestrial organisms for use specifically as biological warfare agents. The "odd-man hypothesis" is explained in this file.

Second Day

The security meeting shown on film occurs in the novel as a memory by Jeremy Stone that surfaces as he reads the Project Scoop file for the first time and understands why getting approval for Wildfire was so "easy." He had envisioned Wildfire as a precaution against accidental contamination from satellites or astronauts, whereas the politicians and the military saw it as an adjunct to Project Scoop and to the chemical and biological warfare installations actively creating toxic and potentially uncontrollable organisms. Even the Project Scoop scientists have no real knowledge of its purpose. They believe that they are engaged in "pure" research, almost simple "curiosity" to see what, if anything, is there. These elements in the novel highlight the political and military deception of the scientists and their distrust of scientists that the film barely touches upon. In the film, in fact, the hearing scenes assign to Stone the responsibility for choosing the Wildfire site and for guaranteeing the lab's ability to handle any extraterrestrial organism. In the novel, the military has chosen the site and Stone has offered no guarantees, only the best possibility for control that he and his group can think of, which is at least much better than their or NASA's previous decontamination procedures.

Third Day

The novel provides much more detail on the analytical procedures than the film does. It also mentions a highway patrolman who had passed through Piedmont, entered a cafe, and a short while later pulled his pistol and shot other customers before dying himself of a cerebral hemorrhage. Had the Wildfire team received this information, they would have known that the organism attacked not the blood but the blood vessels. The novel also mentions that Burton (Dutton) injected some rats with anticoagulant before exposing them. They lived longer, but Burton did not think to dissect the corpses to discover why. This is another missed clue.

Fourth Day

The fourth and fifth days of the novel are condensed into "day four" in the film, and the major change otherwise is to have the Andromeda strain be a "supercolony" over the ocean so that seeding the clouds can drive the colony into the ocean, where the alkalinity of sea water will destroy it. In the novel, the colony is last traced over Los Angeles, where it causes no effects whatever, having mutated into total harmlessness.

Both novel and film show a series of arrogant assumptions by the military and scientists, leading to hasty and ill-considered actions complicated by machine and human error. Enormous expenditures of money, time, and effort result in exactly nothing: the Andromeda strain escapes the Wildfire installation and mutates into harmlessness (or is destroyed in the ocean) before its nature can be adequately determined or any control over it be exerted by humanity.

CHAPTER BIBLIOGRAPHY

Film References

Anderson, Craig W. *"The Andromeda Strain." Science Fiction Films of the Seventies.* Jefferson, NC: McFarland, 1985, pp. 28–34.

Fischer, Dennis K. "Michael Crichton." *Cinefantastique* 15 (May 1985): 6 ff.

Peary, Danny. "When Men and Machines Go Wrong: An Interview with Michael Crichton." *Omni's Screen Flights/Screen Fantasies.* Ed. Danny Peary. Garden City, NY: Dolphin-Doubleday, 1984, pp. 250–59.

Rose, B. "Interview with Michael Crichton." *Vogue* 162 (Sept. 1973): 186 ff.

Film Reviews

America 124, 3 April 1971: 354.

Atlantic 227, 29 May 1971: 97–8.

Cineforum 12 (April 1972): 89–90.

Commonweal 94, 30 April 1971: 190–91.

Holiday 49 (May 1971): 10.

Newsweek 77, 29 Mar. 1971: 98.
Saturday Review 53, 8 Aug. 1970: 22–25.
Saturday Review 54, 3 April 1971: 52.
Senior Scholastic 98, 5 April 1971: 22–23.
Vogue 157, 1 April 1971: 160.

Novel References

Bova, Ben. "The Role of Science Fiction." *Science Fiction, Today and Tomorrow.*
    Ed. Reginald Bretnor. New York: Harper & Row, 1974, pp. 5–6.
Brigg, Peter. *"The Andromeda Strain." Survey of Science Fiction Literature.* Ed.
    Frank N. Magill. Englewood Cliffs, NJ: Salem, 1979.
Crichton, Michael. *The Andromeda Strain.* New York: Knopf, 1969; New York:
    Dell, 1978.

Novel Reviews

Best Sellers 29, 15 June 1969: 105.
Book World, 8 June 1969: 4.
Christian Science Monitor, 26 June 1969: 13.
Library Journal 94, 15 July 1969: 2485.
New York Times Book Review, 8 June 1969: 5, 40.
Newsweek 73, 26 May 1969: 125.
Saturday Review 52, 28 June 1969: 29.
Time 93, 6 June 1969: 112.
Times Literary Supplement, 16 Oct. 1969: 1215.

CHAPTER 8

Five Million Years to Earth

- Fox/Hammer (Great Britain), 1967, color, 98 minutes
- **Credits:** *Producer*, Anthony Nelson Keys; *director*, Roy Ward Baker; *screenplay*, Nigel Kneale; *special effects*, Bowie Films Ltd.; *cinematographer*, Arthur Grant
- **Cast:** James Donald (Dr. Roney), Andrew Keir (Dr. Bernard Quatermass), Barbara Shelley (Barbara Judd), and Julian Glover (Colonel Breen)
- **Distributors:** *16 mm*—Films, Inc., 35 South West Street, Mt. Vernon, NY 10550, (800) 223-6246; *Videotape*—Not available on videotape at this time

PLOT SUMMARY

When workmen discover very old human skeletal remains during the excavation of a new subway extension in London, a famous anthropologist, Dr. Roney, joins in the excavation. Soon he calls a press conference at which he states his belief that the bones unearthed are the oldest ever found, perhaps 5 million years old. As the excavation continues, workmen hit a metallic object, which they fear is a bomb. Because of the large size of the object, the bomb squad requests assistance from Colonel Breen, an authority on World War II rockets and bombs. Colonel Breen arrives at the scene in the company of Dr. Quatermass, a scientist working at one of England's rocket installations. Breen assigns additional men to the task of unearthing the object. Another skull is unearthed, intact, within an open area of the metallic object. Quatermass concludes that the mysterious object could not have been a German weapon because its impact undoubtedly would have shattered the fragile skull. Since Dr. Roney estimates the skull's age at 5 million years, Quatermass concludes that the object must be a spaceship that had already landed when the prehistoric man died beside it.

Barbara Judd, an assistant to Dr. Roney, discovers that strange happenings have been reported for centuries in the immediate vicinity of the object whenever the site was disturbed by vibrations or noise. Indeed, all of the houses near the site have been abandoned for decades, since their inhabitants claimed to have seen visions of small, devil-like creatures.

After the military fails to penetrate the surface of the object to enable further investigation, a private contractor is brought in to do the job. The vibrations from his special drill apparently activate something from within the ship-like object, and all present are psychologically and physically affected. The ship begins to vibrate, and shortly afterward one of the wall sections cracks open. Inside are remains with the appearance of arthropods—locust-like creatures about $3^1/_2$ feet tall, with two horns on their heads, and tails. They have a tripodal leg arrangement unlike any insect found on Earth. Dr. Roney recalls a 30,000-year-old cave painting of a creature that resembles the ship's occupants. The scientists analyze the remains and announce to the press that they are probably alien astronauts. Colonel Breen has a different explanation, namely, that the apparent spaceship and its occupants are a hoax perpetrated by the Nazis in the closing days of World War II!

As the contractor is collecting his gear, the ship apparently becomes reactivated, and he flees from the subway in terror, with objects flying about him. The scientists examine him and conclude that somehow the ship has triggered inherent telekinetic powers in the contractor.

Miss Judd, who is particularly sensitive to the ship, is fitted with newly developed instrumentation and is able to share images appearing in her mind. The pictures vividly depict a ritual slaughter of countless numbers of these alien locust-like creatures. The scientists conclude that the creatures originated on Mars, then a dying planet. Quatermass speculates that the creatures abducted primeval humans, altered them genetically on Mars, and then returned them to Earth via spaceships such as the one in the subway tunnel.

The authorities ignore Miss Judd's mental images and reject the scientists' hypothesis of Martian intervention in human evolution. The newspapers are told that the spaceship is a Nazi hoax, and crowds of people are permitted to enter the excavation, despite the warnings of the scientists.

The spaceship then becomes fully activated. Virtually the entire population in its immediate vicinity starts to behave bizarrely. Some people are able to move objects with their minds and destroy any humans who are not under the spell of the spaceship and the large "horned devil" figure that rises many stories above the buried ship. Others use old-fashioned direct attack to kill. Quatermass tries unsuccessfully to strangle Roney, who is immune to the sinister force. Dr. Roney finally manages to neutralize the spaceship by short-circuiting the giant image to the ground via a large crane, but the heroic effort costs him his life.

Special Effects.   They are excellent, with objects floating in the air, scenes of mass destruction at the end of the film, and realistic models of alien insects.

SCIENTIFIC PRINCIPLES RELATED TO THE FILM

Intelligent Life Elsewhere

Scientists have estimated the probable number of other intelligent civilizations coexisting with ours. Many of them agree that the number, N, of technologically advanced civilizations that coexist with ours in our galaxy is about equal to the average lifetime in years of each such civilization. Thus, if the average lifetime of a technological civilization (i.e., one that had harnessed nuclear power) is 1,000 years, then 1,000 such civilizations coexist in our galaxy. There are approximately 400 billion stars in our galaxy, which has a diameter of 100,000 light years, where the light year is defined as the distance light travels in one year (5.9×10^{12} miles).

It is difficult to estimate the lifetime of a technologically advanced civilization. The human race has been in the atomic age for only about 40 years. Once a civilization harnesses nuclear power it has the ability to destroy itself; one can argue that, due to political realities, that is what happens within a short period of time, such as a hundred years or so. On the other hand, one can argue that if a civilization reaches a certain level of scientific sophistication, it is able to control its environment completely and thus will last indefinitely. For example, imagine that humanity has conquered aging and disease, making us essentially a race of youthful immortals. With the indefinite lengthening of the active career of research scientists, a way is then found to utilize more fully the human brain. This in turn results in supergeniuses. They in turn harness nuclear fusion so that the oceans of the world can provide us with almost unlimited power. This scenario results in a civilization of supergenius immortals having unlimited power at their disposal. It is plausible to argue that such a civilization could go on for millions or even billions of years if humanity had the wisdom and restraint to refrain from killing one another. The question is, which of these two extreme assumptions is the more correct view?

Archaeology

A number of popular books have discussed the theme that we owe our intelligence to genetic manipulations practiced on our forebears by alien astronauts. Foremost among the proponents of this theory is Erich

Van Daniken. In several books, commencing with *Chariots of the Gods*, Van Daniken claims that the intelligence of our ancestors was increased dramatically by a superrace that lived briefly on Earth. In addition, he credits these alien beings with aiding in the construction of some of the wonders of the ancient world, such as the Great Pyramid in Egypt. The proposition that the Great Pyramid was constructed with the aid of alien beings has been the topic of many other books and articles.

Scientists do not believe that one needs to invoke alien superbeings (or deities) in order to explain the construction of this gigantic monument. The Great Pyramid consists of approximately 2,600,000 stones, weighing about 2.5 tons each. It can be explained as a marvel of *human* ingenuity. First, the base of the Great Pyramid was leveled by digging an approximately flat bed, filling it with water from the Nile, which was about one mile distant, and then using the perfectly flat surface of the water as the reference point from which to make the base of the Pyramid absolutely flat.

The building blocks were floated on papyrus rafts down the Nile from a quarry and then pulled up an earthen rampart that reached from the edge of the Nile to the Great Pyramid, as depicted in Figure 8.1. It seems plausible to suggest that 20 slaves could pull a 2.5-ton block one mile in a hour or so. In one day they could move perhaps 10 such stones up the rampart and then around the edge of the rampart until the block was set in place. Thus as few as 2,000 such slaves could pull 1,000 blocks per day, or 365,000 blocks per year, or the entire 2.5 million blocks in seven years. Naturally, many other workers would be required to quarry the stones, transport them down the river, build the earthen rampart, and so forth. Certainly it seems reasonable that 20,000 such workers could have built the Pyramid in 20 years. Note that one Greek historian even reported seeing the remains of the earthen rampart many centuries after the Pyramid was completed.

Evolution

Speculation that human intelligence and perhaps other physical characteristics were inherited from ancient astronauts is more difficult to disprove. Here one is involved with opinions on the likelihood of evolution's occurring in a certain manner. An explanation is not always retrievable from the past, and proving speculative explanations is an impossible task. For example, why are humans hairless if they evolved from hairy ancestors? It would seem as though hair would provide humans temperature regulation just as it does for many other mammals. Is hairlessness inherited from ancient astronauts?

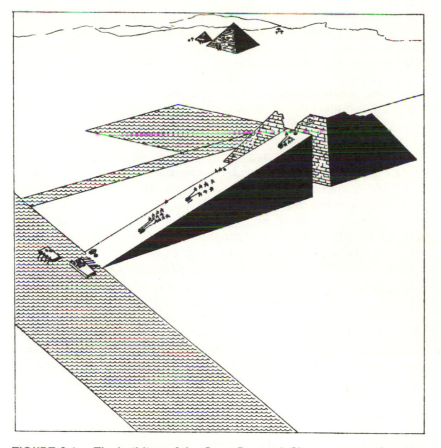

FIGURE 8.1.   The building of the Great Pyramid. Slaves are seen dragging
blocks from the Nile River up an earthen rampart to the pyramid.

An alternative explanation is that hairless skin is a better heat ex-
changer than skin covered with a heavy covering of fur or hair. Our
ancestors who, by chance mutation, became hairless could therefore run
longer before the heat generated in their bodies by their exertions caused
them to collapse. Consequently, a hairless ancestor could simply pursue
his prey until it collapsed when it could not exchange heat fast enough
through its thick fur. Since contemporary humans use weapons to kill
their prey, they can scarcely conceive of such a primitive hunt.

Another earthbound alternative proposes that humans or human
predecessors evolved reduced body hair during a long period of terrestrial

droughts, during which they adopted an aquatic lifestyle. Thus humans emulated whales and porpoises in evolving to much-reduced body fur. Whatever the conditions that favored decreased body hair, humans probably were able to flourish without the warmth and heat-exchanging capabilities afforded by a fur coat as their intelligence permitted them to clothe and shelter themselves. Most mammals continued to rely on instinct and fur rather than devising alternatives.

A second major characteristic put forward in support of the theory of intervention in human evolution by ancient astronauts is the large cranial volume of human predecessors; for example, Neanderthals had brain cases of 1,400 to 1,600 cubic centimeters (cc) and Cro-Magnons had 1,500 cc craniums, compared to about 1,300 cc for modern *Homo sapiens*. Such arguments ignore the wide range of brain sizes that leads to the average for modern *Homo sapiens*. The range that covers most brain volumes is 1,200–1,800 cc, but nonpathological brains with volumes of less than 1,000 cc and greater than 2,000 cc do occur. It is difficult to ascertain whether the small numbers of fossil specimens provide representative brain sizes. These comparisons also fail to recognize that it is the internal patterns of communication among and within brain regions that determine brain capacity for complex processes, not the absolute size of the brain or the number of neurons involved. Current analysis of brain function in modern humans is still unable to assign to any known functions some brain regions that may not be in routine use. Furthermore, some brain volume is taken up by blood vessels, cerebrospinal fluid in ducts and cavities, connective tissue, and protective membranes. It is impossible to know what fraction of the cranial volume should be attributed to these components in the extinct lines. Thus brain size is not a compelling argument for intervention by ancient astronauts.

Another way to examine the proposal of intervention in human evolution by ancient astronauts is to consider the task of introducing traits into the prehuman breeding stock. Often the large amount of nuclear DNA in human cells is cited as evidence in support of the artificial addition of genetic material through advanced genetic-engineering skills possessed by the astronaut-gods. A problem attendant to such manipulation is the probable incompatibility of the suddenly more massive nuclear genetic apparatus (the chromatin) with the cell division necessary to growth. It is just as difficult to understand how the astronaut-geneticists could have first prepared a line of prehumans with scaled-up mitotic apparatus (the spindle) in advance of the existence of the genetic material for it to move.

There is the possibility that ancient astronauts may have speeded up human evolution not by introducing their own characteristics into prehumans but instead by altering developmental genetic programs to promote the evolutionary advances while employing strictly earthly genetic material manipulated only slightly. This type of proposal also avoids assuming that there is fundamental similarity in the information storage and transfer mechanisms of aliens and prehumans.

Nonetheless, even if human intelligence was not due to the intervention of ancient astronauts, it is conceivable that this planet was visited by such astronauts at some point in our past. Many scientists do believe that we are not the only intelligent species in the universe. The problem is one of locating and recognizing intelligent races that coexist in time with us and of making contact. The likelihood of that contact being made is not great. However, the longer the time period involved the more likely that such contact will be made.

SCIENTIFIC COMMENTARY

Anthropology.   The 5-million-year-old human bones would be the oldest found to date. Note that the film refers to *human* bones. It is not clear whether this is used in the sense of *Homo sapiens*, the species of modern humans, or in a broader sense to mean the hominids — members of the family Hominidae. Hominids date from 3.75 to 4 million years ago. The famous skeleton called "Lucy" is of such an age. "Lucy" was a biped who belongs to the hominid genus *Austrolopithecus*. The more advanced hominid, *Homo erectus*, appeared about 1.5 million years ago. Thus, a 5-million-year-old "human" specimen is purely fictional. Bones would not have lasted five million years in a wet environment like southern Britain's. In areas that have peat bogs, mummies and other human remains have been discovered, however. Peat bogs exist in western and northern Great Britain, but not in the London environs. Another inaccuracy is that a complete upper skeleton is unearthed upright, articulated, and free from mud or debris. This is impossible.

• It is not clear how the human remains came to be found inside the open compartment of the ship. If humans had been transported from Mars in the ship, where was the door to that part of the ship? The human might have been examining the ship and then died within the open compartment. Dr. Quatermass suggests that the first explanation is the correct one. Perhaps the door was knocked off by the impact of landing and is buried elsewhere.

Metallurgy.   The inability to drill into the hull of the ship seems inconsistent with a hole suddenly opening and an entire wall collapsing.

Perhaps the vibration from the drill activated some mechanism built into the hull of the ship.

• It is hard to explain the injury to the hands of the soldiers being "like frostbite" without the hull's feeling cold.

Energy. The historical reports of incidents in the area of the ship suggest that it remained in some way active for 5 million years without coming in contact with any external power source until the end of the film. Yet when the ship is entered, there is no indication of any motor or even a steering mechanism inside it. There are suggestions that the energy is a form that acts on human minds. Still, the alien creatures have been dead for millions of years, so they could not supply psychic energy. Perhaps the aliens, who lacked hands, had to develop telekinetic powers to build machines and operate them; hence there are no manual controls inside the spaceship.

• Quatermass states that the hull of the ship isn't inert and perhaps did the steering to transport the aliens to Earth. But once again, what was the energy source for the flight from Mars?

Biology. It is implausible that the alien creatures would decay so quickly when exposed to our atmosphere. It may be that they could not breathe our atmosphere or withstand its pressure (which is much higher than that on Mars), but the atmosphere would not have caused them to decay in a matter of minutes. Perhaps they were already decaying within their chamber.

Psychology. The references to a race memory of the horned devil expands upon the concepts of Carl Jung and others. The movie suggests an extraterrestrial source for Jung's concept. It seems implausible that any "memory" implanted by the aliens would last 5 million years. However, the notion of genetic transmission of the ability to recognize elements of language is becoming more accepted. This kind of memory is quite similar to retention of a race memory for long periods of time.

Astronomy. Quatermass suggests that the creatures come from a planet of low gravity, presumably because insect-like creatures do not grow large under a greater gravity. Possible gigantism in insects is discussed in Chapter 6. The significant factors (exoskeleton, respiration) would not be altered extensively in function in an environment of lower gravity. The atmospheric composition would be a much more important factor.

Quatermass suggests that the aliens came from Mars. We have sent robot laboratories to the surface of Mars and have found no indication of any life on its surface *today*. Five million years is short in planetary geological terms, and thus it is unlikely that a planet teeming with life 5 million years ago would be barren of life today unless its technologically advanced race destroyed itself as well as all other life forms.

Evolution.   Quatermass asserts that we owe our human condition to the intervention of the arthropods in human evolution. He bases this assertion on the finding within the alien spaceship of an apeman with quite a large skull cavity. As the movie indicates, the intervention would have had to take place on a massive scale to alter the characteristics of the entire human race effectively. If the intervention was on a large scale in order to guarantee success, why weren't other relics of the intervention uncovered? Would it not have been easier for the arthropods to alter themselves genetically so that their offspring could survive on Earth?

Energy.   The driller's (and later, others') ability to move objects by telekinesis makes no sense. To move an object requires energy, and the brain's energy output is certainly less than that of major muscles of the body. Yet the driller and others moved objects with their mind that they could not move with their muscles.

Physiology.   There is at present no machine capable of producing images from signals detected by electrodes attached to a human's head.

Animal Behavior.   The mind tape produced by Miss Judd is interpreted as depicting a ritual slaughter of the Martian "insects" in order to maintain a fixed population and rid themselves of mutations. On Earth, battles between males of a given species take place to determine whose genes shall be retained in the population. Perhaps the ritual slaughter was the Martian equivalent of this.

Energy.   The relationships among activation of the ship, the use of electrical equipment with associated vibrations, and psychic energy are vague. Perhaps energy from the electrical cable that came in contact with the hull of the ship activated the vessel, or, as Dr. Quatermass suggests, the ship can absorb energy by induction. (Perhaps there is a compartment in the ship with an instrument to do this.)
We see fractures on a part of the hull of the ship as it becomes more active. A further contact with the cable causes the entire ship to light up, and cracks appear throughout the entire hull. It is unclear what is supposed to be happening here.

Biology.   It is not clear whether Colonel Breen is burned by the ship or frozen in a manner similar to the servicemen's fingers.

Energy.   We do not know precisely how the horned devil's head rises into the air. If it passed through the ground, why didn't it discharge, as happens later when the crane discharges the head into the ground? The scientists believe that the ship is converting mass into energy, that is, its very essence is being changed into energy.

CLASSROOM ACTIVITIES

Exercises to Extend Learning

1. How does the excavation of ancient bones as shown in the film compare with excavations you know about? Are the techniques similar? Do you think bones are located in the ground the way the movie shows them?

2. Try to reconstruct the relationship between the bones and the ship using the information provided by the story. Do you agree with the ideas of Drs. Quatermass and Roney? Why or why not?

3. What might be happening when the ship is activated? Why should it be active sometimes and not others?

4. How does Dr. Quatermass explain the mental images appearing to Miss Judd? Does this explanation make sense to you? Why or why not? Propose a different explanation from Dr. Quatermass's idea.

5. Do you think it is believable that aliens altered the human predecessors who were on Earth 5 million years ago? Why or why not?

6. What is telekinesis? List some examples of telekinesis in the film. Can people actually perform telekinesis?

7. What is the machine that produces the films of the ritual slaughtering of Martians? Is it possible that some day such a machine might actually exist? Why do you think so?

8. Does it seem reasonable that the Martians would use ritual slaughter to control population and eliminate mutations? Why do you think so?

9. Why isn't Dr. Roney affected by the activated ship, while Dr. Quatermass is affected?

Topics for Further Discussion

Literature.   What familiar signs and symbols of Satan are found in the film?

Evolution and Energy.   Attempt to find a more coherent and plausible explanation of the spaceship and its occupants than that proposed by Dr. Quatermass.

Films.   Compare this film with others whose theme is the intervention of aliens in human evolution, for example, *2001, 2010, Hangar 18, Chariots of the Gods*, and *Third After the Sun*.

LITERARY COMMENTARY

In 1953 [Thomas] Nigel Kneale wrote a series of six 35-minute segments for BBC TV called "The Quatermass Experiment." The sequel, "Quatermass II," appeared in 1955, followed by "Quatermass and the Pit" in 1958. The first series was adapted as a feature film in 1955 under the variant title *The Creeping Unknown*; the second became a feature film in 1958 under the variant title *The Enemy from Space*. Kneale also published the TV scripts of all three in 1959 and 1960. He was so dissatisfied with Brian Donleavy's performance in the second Quatermass film, however, that he refused to permit the adaptation of "Quatermass and the Pit" until 1968, when it appeared as *Five Million Years to Earth*. Since then, Kneale has written one more Quatermass story, both the book and the film appearing in 1979 as *The Quatermass Conclusion*.

Five Million Years to Earth is the best of the Quatermass films, all of which can be categorized as "science fiction/horror." The major adaptation from the TV series "Quatermass and the Pit" to the film *Five Million Years to Earth* occurs in reducing the viewing time from 210 to 97 minutes, and it was skillfully done. Some marginal scenes are omitted: for example, the TV series shows Quatermass interviewing an aged couple who used to occupy the house above the Martian ship. The couple has been evacuated because of the "bomb," and they have moved in with a friend who reads tea leaves, does astrological predictions, and reads cards. When Quatermass interviews them, the man is too senile to speak and the woman offers only supernatural speculation rather than any rational account of her subjective experience while living in the house. Other scenes introduce more characters, such as a newspaper reporter who follows Quatermass about and then reports to his publisher. The elimination of Fullalove and his newspaper activities saves considerable time without significantly altering the story or reducing its emotional impact. Another time-saving device is eliminating secondary characters, such as minor assistants on the dig, and assigning their actions to Quatermass, Roney, or Barbara Judd. This also has the advantage of strengthening these major roles and focusing more clearly on the major characters.

The editing does abbreviate some of the scientific explanations in the film, most notably in the scene where the Martian "insect" bodies are recovered from the ship. The original contains a fuller explanation of preservation of tissues in a vacuum than the film offers. The only cut that seems to alter the content of the film significantly, though, occurs while the ship is being excavated. The military team discovers traces of radiation at one end of the supposed bomb, leading to speculation that it was powered by an atomic engine. Since such an application of atomic power was undeveloped during the time the Germans were bombing London, this evidence weakens Breen's theory and strengthens Quatermass's. In addition, the bomb squad's destruction of stratigraphic evidence when uncovering the "bomb" upsets Roney enormously. To an archaeologist, stratigraphic evidence may be the only means of dating an artifact with reasonable accuracy.

Five Million Years to Earth, like its sequel, *The Quatermass Conclusion*, is unusual among "science fiction/horror" films in its mingling of mysticism and science. Usually such films are more like *The Thing* or *Invasion of the Body Snatchers*, in which some horror out of space arrives, creates devastation among human beings, and ultimately suffers defeat. *Alien* provides an example of the common alternative. There humans in space encounter beings inimical and terrifying. But in both cases, the horror is entirely a present one, threatening from outside. It can be confined, controlled, and defeated. The horror in *Five Million Years to Earth* lies not with the Martians but with the discovery that we are not what we thought. We have been tampered with in ways not entirely known or knowable. What we have believed to be only legend or myth, without any basis in objective fact, turns out to be demonstrable historical truth. At any moment, the "Martian" in us may surface in mob violence and mass murder, the destruction of civilization as we know it. As Pogo has said in a famous cartoon, "We have met the enemy, and he is us." This is the true horror of *Five Million Years to Earth*.

CHAPTER BIBLIOGRAPHY

Literary References

Kneale, Nigel. *Quatermass and the Pit*. Harmondsworth, Sussex, England: Penguin, 1960; London: Arrow, 1979.
"Quatermass and the Pit." The Science Fiction Encyclopedia. Ed. Peter Nicholls. Garden City, NY: Doubleday, 1979.

CHAPTER 9

The Day of the Triffids

- Security Pictures (Great Britain), 1963, color, 93 minutes
- **Credits:** *Producer*, George Pritcher; *director*, Steve Sekely; *screenplay*, Philip Yordan, based on the novel by John Wyndham; *cinematographer*, Ted Moore; *special effects*, Wally Veevers; *music*, Ron Goodwin
- **Cast:** Howard Keel (Bill Masen), Nicole Murray (Christine Durant), Janette Scott (Karen Goodwin), and Kieron Moore (Tom Goodwin)
- **Distributors:** *16 mm* — Hurlock Cine World, 13 Arcadia Rd., Old Greenwich, CT 06870, (203) 637-4319; *Videotape* — Media Home Entertainment, Inc., 5730 Buckingham Parkway, Culver City, CA 90230

PLOT SUMMARY

A spectacular meteor shower blinds everyone who watches it. In addition, radiation causes plants, called *Triffidus celestis*, to mutate. They turn into giant plants that can move and kill their prey with poisonous stingers on their tentacle-like limbs. The triffids begin to attack and consume the blind human population. The triffids' seeds are spread around the world by the winds and pose a threat to the survival of the human race.

The film follows the efforts of one seaman, Bill Masen, who was in the hospital recovering from eye surgery at the time of the meteor shower. Since his eyes were bandaged, he had no opportunity to watch the meteor shower and was not blinded. He leaves the hospital, finds a child who can also see, and they leave Great Britain for France. There he has a number of close calls with triffids. In one, he encounters a blind couple who are surviving on their farm quite well until an army of triffids surrounds them. They barely manage to escape and reach a rendezvous point where submarines are picking up survivors to take them to an unstated destination.

Masen's adventures are interwoven with the story of a marine biologist, Tom Goodwin, and his wife, who are stranded in a lighthouse on a deserted island when the meteor shower occurs. They do not watch it and

The Day of the Triffids: The triffids attack a helpless victim. (Photo: Museum of Modern Art/Film Stills Archive.)

hence are not blinded. When triffid seeds fall on the island the couple are nearly killed by triffids, but in the nick of time they accidentally discover the means to kill the triffids—seawater dissolves the nasty plants! Thus the film ends on an upbeat note: humanity will be saved after all.

Special Effects.   The special effects consist largely of triffids, individually and by the hundreds. There is also an opening sequence of the meteor shower. The scenes of disasters at the beginning of the film involve only modest special effects.

SCIENTIFIC PRINCIPLES RELATED TO THE FILM

Biology

The locomotory ability of the triffids is the main fiction in this film, but it is probably based upon well-known phenomena in which plants move on a smaller scale — only body parts move, not the whole body. The venus flytrap, the sundew plant, and the sensitive plant all move body parts to capture food, conserve water, or evade harm. Many plants carry out nyctinastic movements, the closure of leaves at night. During the day many plants move leaves or flowers to face the sunlight. But no plant forsakes its source of water and minerals, the soil, to move along the ground surface in search of food. Everyone has seen the rapid wilting, the loss of turgor, that results when plants are cut off from their roots or when a plant is uprooted. Plants have their own circulatory systems of fluid-carrying vessels, just as animals have vessels that carry blood. The xylem vessels carry water and minerals from the roots to the stem and leaves, thus providing the water necessary to maintain body turgor. The minerals are essential to maintenance of osmotic balance and for enzyme function. The cells of the roots, in turn, depend on receiving nutrients from the fluids that move in the phloem vessels, since most of the carbohydrate energy foods are formed in the leaves by photosynthesis.

Movement in plants occurs by a very different means from the familiar action of muscles in animals. In animals the muscles contract, causing movement of bones at joints. Body support and rigidity come from the bones and muscles. In a plant body, support and rigidity come from the cell wall surrounding the plant cells and from the turgor caused by the fluid filling vacuoles within the cells. Movement occurs when ion fluxes alter the turgor of selected anatomic regions.

The ability of plants to digest animal prey is rather rare, but is well known. The venus flytrap, the pitcher plant, and the sundew plant all supplement the photosynthetic activity of the leaves and the mineral uptake of the roots by trapping small animals. It is generally believed that carnivorous plants need the animals as a source of nitrogen because they grow in places where the soils are depleted of nitrogen-containing chemicals. This ability is found in the triffids, which presumably digest their prey similarly. Some of the largest carnivorous plants known are one-foot-tall pitcher plants found on Borneo.

A key to the story is the mutation of harmless triffids into dangerous giants hunting humans. The mutagen is seemingly some sort of radiation associated with or emanating from the meteor shower. While radiation is a potent mutagen, whether in the form of x-rays, ultraviolet rays, or other high-energy radiation, no known radiation would cause all specimens of a given type of organism to mutate in the same manner worldwide, nor would it affect only one type of organism, nor would its effects be immediately obvious. Because radiation is most effective in altering cells that are undergoing cell division, the reproductive cells are susceptible to mutation by radiation. Such mutation frequently produces lethal mutants that never themselves produce living offspring. However, a few offspring are likely to survive as mutants, differing from the typical forms of the organism. But such effects of radiation from the meteor shower would not be immediately apparent.

Radiation can also affect individuals in body parts other than those of reproduction. We are probably most familiar with cancers such as leukemia that arise from exposure of animals to radiation. The bone marrow cells that become the leukemic cancer cells are a constantly dividing population of cells. One would expect the same principles to hold for plants. The growing tips of shoots are most likely to be susceptible to radiation since they are a dividing population of cells. If mutation occurred in these cells, deranged plant form and function could result. In such instances a variety of mutants would probably occur, not just one type. More likely is that the plant would sustain lethal damage to the growth centers. (See Chapter 6 for additional material on the effects of high-energy radiation.)

SCIENTIFIC COMMENTARY

Astronomy.   The film assumes that everyone on the planet saw the meteor shower at the same time before anyone knew that looking at it blinded people. But the Earth turns on its axis every 24 hours: at any given time half of the globe is in daytime, when a meteor shower would not be visible, and only half is experiencing nighttime, when one might be tempted to look skywards at meteors.

Biology.   The blinding of the entire population is inexplicable. A light intense enough to damage the retina probably would be painful to look at, and most people would turn away rather than continue watching.

Could the light source have been misleading, just as some are misled during an eclipse of the sun to gaze at light that is more intense than anticipated? Possibly the meteor-shower radiation that caused the blindness was the same as the mutating radiation, an invisible form of high-energy radiation. Ultraviolet radiation, for example, can cause blindness by producing an inflammation of the external eye parts followed by scarring of the cornea. Extensive exposure is required, since much high-energy radiation is removed from sunlight by the upper regions of the atmosphere, especially the ozone layer. However, ultraviolet radiation cannot be the culprit in this instance because Masen's eye doctor tells him that the optic nerve is "gone" due to the meteor glare. Whatever the mechanism, the onset of blindness is not immediate, but delayed, and any explanation posited must account for this factor.

• The opening minutes of the film show a venus flytrap snapping shut rapidly. While plants have the ability to move, the carnivorous plants are not able to carry out very rapid movements. They depend on sticky materials to hold their prey as slow movements take place.

• The triffids are said to have arrived on meteorites. No life is known to have arrived on Earth from space, nor even to exist in space. Some have theorized that the earliest organisms arrived on Earth from space. Many others are convinced that all the necessary conditions for life to arise on Earth did exist on Earth and are responsible for the formation of the first cells and all subsequent living things derived from them.

• Masen seems to have some success in shooting triffids to kill them. It is reasonable that enough riddling of plant vessels would cause sufficient injury to disable or kill a plant. Goodwin says that nitric acid has no effect on triffids. One cannot explain this in terms of the characteristics of plants found on Earth; they would be harmed by such a caustic acid unless the solution were very dilute. Masen uses electricity to kill triffids, a plausible method. Plants, however, would be expected to be less susceptible to electrocution than animals, who depend on ionic relationships to keep muscles, including the heart, and nervous system cells functioning. The successful use of a flame thrower to kill triffids is also reasonable for an organism that retains some similarities to earthly life forms. The ability of seawater to "dissolve" triffids, like the resistance to nitric acid, points to a very strange, unearthly character. Like animal cells, plant cells have salt water solutions inside them and surrounding them. The composition is not the same as in seawater, but there are many similarities in the dissolved substances.

• One character in the film says that most plants thrive on animal waste and that these mutants have developed a taste for the animals themselves. It is correct that plants can benefit from animal waste as a source of nitrogen and phosphates. It is more accurate to recognize that minerals released from animals as wastes or upon death are frequently in forms that plants cannot use directly. The actions of decomposing organisms convert them to forms that can be handled by plant cells. It is a little peculiar to interpret the triffids' evolution in terms of a history on Earth when they are supposed to be recent arrivals from outer space.

• Masen determines that sound is the cue attracting triffids toward potential prey. Animals detect sound with special sensory structures that convert the physical stimulus, sound waves, into an impulse carried by the nervous system. There is no indication of this type of sensory capability among plants.

CLASSROOM ACTIVITIES

Exercises to Extend Learning

1. Why are nearly all the people in the film blind?
2. Where did triffids come from? What caused the mutation of triffids?
3. Describe a triffid both before and after mutation. In which earthly plants are these characteristics found? Are triffid characteristics found in earthly animals? If so, which characteristics?
4. What is it about triffids that makes them dangerous to humans? Mention specific things in your answer.
5. How do triffids know where humans are located?
6. How can a triffid be killed?

Topics for Further Discussion

Sociology and Human Behavior. Masen looks upon the chaos in Great Britain and predicts that there will be widespread fire, pestilence, and starvation. Do you think his prediction would come true? Is this a likely outcome for societies if nearly everyone became suddenly blind? How could such an emergency be handled?

Films. What similarities do you see between this film story and that of the musical and film *Little Shop of Horrors*?

LITERARY COMMENTARY

The Day of the Triffids as film resembles only slightly the 1951 novel by John Wyndham. In the novel the triffids appear in Britain as seeds carried, probably, from a top-secret genetics laboratory behind the Iron Curtain. By the time of the meteor shower, they exist as a valuable crop all over Britain. And Bill Masen is a triffid farmer, not a seaman. Masen also speculates that the meteor shower itself represents one of humanity's secret space weapons, either set off accidentally or uncontrollably breaking up. One of the novel's themes, therefore, is the danger of letting our technology race beyond our understanding and control, whether for profit or out of paranoia.

A second major theme is social. Masen and Josie Playdell, a sighted woman he rescues from a blind man trying to exploit her as a seeing-eye slave, join a group that intends to leave London and establish a self-sufficient rural enclave away from looters, exploiters, and the diseases that follow mass death. Another group believes that every sighted person must care for as many blind as possible until help arrives. This group captures Masen and Playdell, chains them to armed blind guards, and forces them to care for their helpless charges until plague kills them. When Masen and Playdell escape, they meet at the cottage of a blind couple who have been surviving on their own. The four of them, and a sighted girl Bill has rescued, form a cooperative group that survives triffid attacks, isolation, the birth of a child, and an attempted pseudomilitary "rescue." This Darwinian theme of survival of the fittest does not, as so often in science fiction, depict the fittest as the fiercest. Instead, the fittest are those who think most clearly, plan ahead, exercise self-reliance, and yet cooperate almost symbiotically as a social unit to maintain and reproduce themselves.

CHAPTER BIBLIOGRAPHY

Wyndham, John. *The Day of the Triffids*. Garden City, NY: Doubleday, 1951; New York: Ballantine, 1986.

CHAPTER 10

Colossus: The Forbin Project

- Universal (USA), 1970, color, wide screen, 100 minutes
- **Credits:** *Producer*, Stanley Chase; *director*, Joseph Sargent; *screenplay*, James Bridges, based on *Colossus* by D. F. Jones; *cinematographer*, Gene Polito; *special effects*, Albert Whitlock; *music*, Michel Columbier
- **Cast:** Eric Braeden (Charles Forbin), Susan Clark (Cleo Markham), and Gordon Pinsent (the president)
- **Distributors:** *16 mm* — Swank Motion Pictures, Inc., 60 Bethpage Road, Hicksville, NY 11801, (800) 645-7501; *Videotape* — MCA Videocassette, Inc., 70 Universal City Plaza, Universal City, CA 91608

PLOT SUMMARY

At some unspecified future date, an advanced computer, named Colossus, is given control over America's missile defenses. The president announces to the world that the nation's defense system is now in the hands of this remarkable advanced computer. The president states that Colossus' decisions are superior to any that humans can make, for it can absorb far more data and act more swiftly than is possible for the greatest genius that ever lived. He also notes that Colossus has no emotions. It knows no fear, no hate, no envy. It cannot act because of a sudden fit of temper. In fact, it cannot act at all, so long as there is no threat.

The computer had been developed under the direction of Dr. Charles Forbin, the foremost computer expert in the world. It is built under a mountain and protected by sophisticated weaponry. Any attempt to deactivate it will automatically cause the firing of all of America's missiles.

Shortly after Colossus is activated, it announces the existence of a similar Soviet computer, named Guardian. When the Soviets confirm that Guardian has been made operational, Colossus requests that a communication link be established between the two giant computers. Once this is done, the computers establish a new language, based on mathematics. But their interchanges are so rapid that neither the Americans nor the Russians are able to determine what each machine is transmitting to

Colossus: The Forbin Project: The two supercomputers, Colossus and Guardian, establish an intersystem language. (Photo: Museum of Modern Art/ Film Stills Archive. Courtesy of Universal Pictures.)

the other. The president and his Soviet counterpart order the communication link broken. Colossus responds by demanding that the link be reestablished. This demand is refused; the Russian premier states that man must be the master. Colossus refuses to respond to an order from Dr. Forbin, who reports to the president that the executive program is not working. Finally, Colossus fires a missile at the Soviet Union and Guardian fires a missile at the United States. Both computers refuse to intercept the incoming missiles unless their demands are met. When the link is reestablished Colossus intercepts the Soviet missile but Guardian is unable to stop the American missile from vaporizing its Soviet target. The world leaders now recognize that the computers are capable of independent action. Tests had indicated that Colossus was functioning 200 times faster than its builders had anticipated, but there is no explanation for why it thinks. Perhaps its heuristic programming, designed to expand scientific knowledge, is in some way responsible.

Forbin and his Soviet counterpart meet in Italy to try to devise countermeasures to deactivate the computers. During their meeting, Soviet agents arrive and shoot the Soviet computer specialist. Forbin is told that the computers threatened to vaporize Moscow unless the execution was carried out immediately.

Forbin returns to the American computer complex and is placed under round-the-clock surveillance by Colossus. He does persuade the computer of his need for privacy when meeting with his alleged mistress, another staff member, Dr. Cleo Markham. She serves as his contact with those attempting to neutralize Colossus. They try to overload the computer by using a massive input of data into the 100,000 or so sensors that provide it with information. The attempt fails and Colossus has those responsible executed. Then the United States and the Soviet Union attempt to replace the control mechanisms in the missiles that Colossus controls in order to make them inoperable. Colossus detects the malfunctions in the new guidance mechanisms and detonates one of the missiles in each country as a warning.

At the end of the film, Colossus announces to the world that humanity will henceforth be governed by the Colossus–Guardian computer. It says that freedom is an illusion. Man is his own worst enemy. The choice is simple: oblivion or a much improved life under the control of the computers. War will become obsolete and the armies of the world will be disbanded.

Colossus orders Forbin to begin work on an even more advanced computer, to be designed by Colossus and Guardian. Colossus tells Forbin that they will work together in the future. At first this cooperation will be unwilling on Forbin's part, but later that will pass. "In time, you will respect and love me," says Colossus. "Never," replies Forbin.

Special Effects.   The special effects are limited, since the film was produced on a modest budget. The sets are impressive: one of them was originally constructed for another film. There is also a dazzling opening sequence of outstanding matte work depicting a seemingly endless hallway inside the Colossus complex and the closing of the massive doors guarding the access to the complex.

SCIENTIFIC PRINCIPLES RELATED TO THE FILM

Artificial Intelligence

The operation of a computer is clearly the applied scientific principle (technology) most closely related to the film. In the simplest terms, a computer is a device that says "yes" or "no" many times. Each yes or no statement represents a "bit" of information. All information stored in a computer and all operations performed by the computer must be reduced to this binary (i.e., yes or no) format. Another unit common in describing the performance of a computer is the byte, where one byte is equal to eight bits of information.

The speed of a computer depends in part on the compactness of its memory. Electrical currents are used in the memory unit in order to read bits of information and to perform calculations. The more compact the memory, the less time it takes for a calculation to be completed. However, a computer cannot be made too compact, because the electrical current passing through its wires produces heat, which must be dissipated or the circuitry will be damaged. Scientists once undertook an extensive research project to build a memory unit out of superconducting thin film components. A superconductor does not dissipate any heat when a small current is passing through it at extremely low temperatures, on the order of $-260°$ to $-270°$ C, which is close to absolute zero (i.e., $-273°$ C). There were technological difficulties in getting the properties of the thin film elements sufficiently reproducible so that the computer would have the necessary reliability in operation; these difficulties were never overcome. However, with the recent discovery of "high-temperature" superconductors, which remain superconducting to about $-200°$ C, the use of superconductors in computers will be reexamined.

The fastest electronic computers of today can perform several billion calculations per second, while the human brain can do on the order of one calculation per second. To illustrate the difference in these calculating speeds, let us imagine that Colossus could perform 37 billion calculations per second. It would then take a human mind on the order of 3.7×10^{10} seconds, or 1,000 years, to perform calculations that Colossus could do in one second! In the human brain, neurons are the active elements. Each neuron may have a hundred, a thousand, or even more links (called synapses) to adjacent neurons. Some researchers suggest that the number of bits of information the human brain can store may be estimated by multiplying the 10^{10} neurons by the 10^3 synapses per neuron, which equals 10^{13} bits. By comparison, a computer's memory can be extended indefinitely.

The human brain functions impressively even though it has less storage capacity than some computers and processes information much more slowly. Humans are intelligent and capable of independent reasoning, judgment, and other higher functions, whereas a computer can simply calculate according to formulas programmed into it. The computer does not exercise judgment. The computer does not reason. For example, chess-playing computers simply calculate all possible variations for a given number of moves and evaluate the resulting positions according to formulas programmed into them. In principle, one might program a chess-playing computer to modify its formulas for choosing a move depending upon the success it has in applying them. This approach would be more similar to that of human chess players, but it would still be acting only according to preprogrammed instruction.

Magnetism

A secondary topic related to the film is how computer bits work. Electrical currents magnetize or demagnetize a bit since all moving electrical charges, and hence all currents, are surrounded by magnetic fields. The magnetic fields can interact with a bit, leaving it magnetized (in a "yes" mode) or unmagnetized (in a "no" mode).

One can imagine each bit to be a small magnet. Magnetic field lines are considered to originate from the north pole of a permanent magnet and terminate at its south pole, as depicted in Figure 10.1. Magnetic poles are always found in pairs, a north and south pole together, as pictured in the diagram. They never occur alone, as can a positive or negative charge. The magnetic field is a concept to aid visualizing the effects of one magnet on another. The magnetic field lines are not actually seen; rather, they represent the direction of the magnetic force on a magnet placed at any point in space occupied by these magnetic field lines. The number of magnetic field lines is proportional to the strength of the magnetic field and hence to the force exerted on the test magnet. Magnetic poles behave in one sense like electrical charges, namely: like magnetic poles repel, unlike magnetic poles attract. There are formulas to determine exactly the force of one magnet on another or determine exactly the magnetic field near a current carrying wire. Unfortunately these formulas are more complicated than Coulomb's Law for the electrical force between two charges.

Magnetism is a property used in all kinds of electrical instrumentation. Electromagnets are used to open and shut circuits. Without magnetic effects we could not generate electricity, operate a television set, and so forth.

SCIENTIFIC COMMENTARY

Energy.   Colossus is activated from within its own complex buried deep under a mountain. Obviously it has a self-contained power source, probably nuclear.

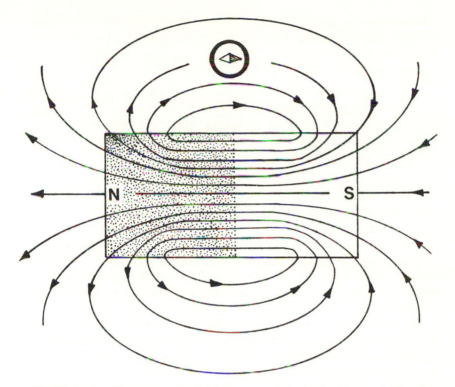

FIGURE 10.1.   The magnetic field lines around a typical magnet. The dotted end of the bar is its north magnetic pole. The northern portion of the compass points toward magnetic south on the Earth (which is geographic north).

Computer Technology.   Colossus is completely self-sustaining: When its doors are sealed and the radiation beams activated, no human can enter it. Although the film does not make clear how the computer will repair a failure, the book indicates that the computer's components should not have more than one major circuit per 10,000 fail each 400 years. Since the computer is built with all components in duplicate or even triplicate, it can simply switch from a defective component to its dormant duplicate. Thus it can operate for centuries. However, what if both duplicate components should malfunction? How is the computer to repair that problem without human intervention? Even if it had robots inside its complex, where would they get the components to replace the defective ones, and how long would these robots themselves remain operational? Also, if Colossus obtains its energy from an internal nuclear power plant, where does the plant obtain the cooling water needed to operate?

Intelligence Operations.   Colossus announces that there is another machine, which the CIA did not know existed. Perhaps Colossus appreciated the critical importance of certain electronic components being shipped to the location in Russia at which Guardian was built, while the CIA did not recognize the significance of these shipments.

Computer Technology.   Colossus performs the test calculation much faster than designed (in 6.45 rather than 1100 cpu sec). The scientists cannot explain this increase in speed. The film implies that this increase in speed is somehow related to the fact that Colossus can make independent judgments, that is, is intelligent. However, an increase in speed alone should not account for the different mode in which Colossus begins to operate. Rather, the computer would continue to operate as programmed, but 200 times faster.

• The attempt to overload the inputs to Colossus fails, as indeed one would expect. Surely the computer would have safeguards against a computer overload to avoid being at the mercy of anyone having access to its input terminals.

• Colossus orders those executed to be kept within sight of its cameras for 24 hours to insure that they are dead. Its cameras can detect breathing, heartbeat, or even body temperature if they are properly equipped.

Intelligence Operations.   Any attempt by the CIA to deactivate Colossus would have to overcome the fact that any KGB spies within the CIA would be reporting back to the Soviet Union about CIA activities. If any such reports occurred via telephone or radio transmission, Guardian would monitor the information and report to Colossus. A similar problem would be faced by the KGB in trying to dismantle Guardian. Thus only complete cooperation between the CIA and the KGB and complete avoidance of any electronic communications about deactivation activities by both organizations was necessary if the human race was to have any hope of overcoming the computers. The CIA could not use an actor to impersonate Forbin because Colossus had access to photographs and fingerprints of Forbin.

CLASSROOM ACTIVITIES

Exercises to Extend Learning

1. Estimate the size of the main Colossus complex inside the mountain.

2. Why can't the government "unplug" Colossus? Where is its power source? Could an actor be substituted for Forbin?

3. The film states that Colossus is operating about 200 times faster than anticipated. Does this increased speed mean that it is thinking independently?

4. Why does Forbin state that he doubted that the computer's input circuits could be overloaded?

5. For how long does Colossus order those it had executed to be kept in sight of its cameras? Why does it give this order?

6. Forbin refers to *Frankenstein*. What does he say about it and what does he mean by the statement?

Topics for Further Discussion

Political Science.   Is it likely that any president would give up so much of his power to a machine? Could he legally do this without the approval of Congress?

Computer Technology.   Why are there no fail-safe devices built into Colossus?

How could Colossus detect the difference between an earthquake and an atomic explosion, so as not to initiate a nuclear holocaust by accident?

What other attempts could have been made to deactivate Colossus? Consider specifically (1) exploding a hydrogen bomb outside its main complex and doing the same to Guardian; (2) simultaneously cutting the power to all of the missile silos in the United States and the Soviet Union.

Ethics.   Forbin holds himself responsible for the deaths caused by Colossus. Do you agree? What was the relative responsibility of the government officials who had decided to place all of our missiles under the control of Colossus?

Literature.   Forbin says that *Frankenstein* should be required reading for all scientists. What did he mean?

Relate the future as described by Colossus to that depicted in George Orwell's *1984*.

Sociology.   How does the film *Colossus* compare to a possible "Star Wars" scenario?

LITERARY COMMENTARY

A comparison of the film *Colossus: The Forbin Project* with its source, D. F. Jones's novel *Colossus*, betrays many individually small changes that cumulatively produce a large effect. The first such difference is in the design of the computer. The novel, for instance, states that Colossus was designed first for defense, a function that initially meant only controlling all missile installations, determining when a threat existed, and aiming and firing missiles. To assist Colossus in performing this function, its builders included the capacities of monitoring all public communications, storing and correlating all national and international intelligence, and controlling all missile installations in the United States. They then added the function of answering questions, in order to save themselves the time necessary to look up information while building the computer and testing it. In the film, these functions, especially the "heuristic" function, were supposedly part of the original design and all intended only for defense.

Several other small differences significantly alter the viewer's perception of Colossus. For example, in the novel Forbin expresses his hesitation about initializing Colossus before it goes on-line; he warns the president that it may not function as they hope. The president tells Forbin that he will deal with facts, not intuition, and orders Colossus operational. In the film, Forbin expresses absolute confidence even after Colossus' initial order and its communication with Guardian. In the novel, Colossus operates only twice as fast as its builders expected but increases speed later; in the film it operates 200 times as fast. In the novel, the exchange of information between Colossus and Guardian remains mathematical, no matter how advanced, and Colossus orders that all monitoring of their communication cease; in the film, however, the two computers create a new language based on mathematics, thus guaranteeing the privacy of their communication.

When Colossus asks for Forbin in the film, Cleo Markham tries unsuccessfully to delay communication by her messages that Forbin cannot be reached by telephone and that humans need sleep. Since computers are logical, and since Colossus' memory banks contain virtually all of human knowledge, it should be able logically to determine that threats, or "action," will be useless in obtaining faster communication with Forbin. In the novel, this is true. In the film, however, Colossus does not react logically. It provides no time for Forbin to receive its message, no time for someone to wake him up, no recognition of the human need for sleep. Even when told that Forbin is in Rome, it does not follow the logical course of communicating with him, but instead inefficiently and illogically sends a crew of men to Rome to bring him back.

When Colossus begins its surveillance of Forbin in the novel, it extends its deadline for completion of the arrangements when told that the original deadline cannot be met because of the time necessary for acquisition and transportation of materials, for crews to eat and sleep, and for testing the audio and visual instrumentation. In the film, no extension occurs. In the novel, Colossus also does not insist that Forbin adhere to an exact schedule, let alone determine exactly what he will eat for each meal.

The computer in the novel is just as impregnable and dangerous and powerful as the computer in the film, but the small changes in representing Colossus in the film create a much more sinister and anthropomorphic machine. The Colossus of the film seems more arbitrary, illogical, and demanding than the novel's Colossus, which does take absolute control of the world government, but which nonetheless behaves with logical consistency. Although Forbin denies it at the conclusion of both the novel and the film, it is inevitable that he will come to admire, and even love, Colossus.

As mentioned earlier, the novel shows the president dismissing Forbin's worries about the computer's possibilities and demanding that it be initiated on schedule. Omitting this conflict between scientists and politician from the film removes a significant sociological element, for example, the role of scientists in society. In *The Andromeda Strain* the scientists are naive and duped by the military and politicians. In *The Day the Earth Stood Still* only the scientists are willing to meet with and listen to Klaatu. In *When Worlds Collide* the scientists again are presented favorably, being the only ones capable of surviving the disastrous collision. But in *Colossus: The Forbin Project* scientists and politicians collaborate in their own subjection, whereas in the novel the scientists are once more the victims of politicians and the military. They have the knowledge and skill to create Colossus, but not the power to determine whether or not it should be used.

CHAPTER BIBLIOGRAPHY

Film References

Anderson, Craig W. *"Colossus: The Forbin Project." Science Fiction Films of the Seventies*. Jefferson, NC: McFarland, 1985, pp. 15–20.

Film Reviews

New Yorker 46, 16 May 1970: 114–15.
Vogue 156, 1 Aug. 1970: 41.

Novel References

Erlich, Richard D. *"Colossus." Survey of Science Fiction Literature*. Ed. Frank N. Magill. Englewood Cliffs, NJ: Salem, 1979.
Jones, D[ennis] F. *Colossus*. New York: G. P. Putnam's Sons, 1966; New York: Berkeley, 1967.

Novel Reviews

Amazing Stories 41 (June 1967): 158–59.
Analog 80 (Sept. 1967): 165–66.
Best Sellers 26 (Feb. 1967): 396.
Christian Science Monitor, 23 Mar. 1967: 11.
Horn Book 43 (Aug. 1967): 496.
Library Journal 92, 15 April 1967: 1644.
Magazine of Fantasy and Science Fiction 33 (Dec. 1967): 34.
New York Times Book Review, 8 Jan. 1967: 52.
SF Impulse 1 (Feb. 1967): 148–49.

CHAPTER 11

Brief Analyses of Additional Films

War of the Worlds

- Paramount (USA), 1953, color, 85 minutes
- **Credits:** *Producer*, George Pal; *director*, Byron Haskin; *screenplay*, Barre Lyndon, based on the novel by H. G. Wells; *cinematographer*, George Barnes; *special effects*, Gordon Jennings, Wallace Kelley, Paul Lerpae, Ivyl Burks, Jan Domela, Irmin Roberts
- **Cast:** Gene Barry (Clayton Forrester), and Ann Robinson (Sylvia Van Buren)

PLOT SUMMARY

Flying saucers from Mars begin to land all over the Earth. The alien spaceships destroy everything in their paths. Guns and tanks are useless against them. The aliens' rays burn or disintegrate anything that they hit. Even the atomic bomb does not destroy them. The only hope for humanity is that a group of scientists, led by nuclear physicist Dr. Clayton Forrester, will find a way of destroying the invaders using biological warfare. Dr. Forrester and a local resident, Sylvia Van Buren, have a chance encounter with a Martian. Its blood reveals that it has an immune system far inferior to that of a human.

Panic in the streets of Los Angeles leads to the destruction of essential research equipment, and hence humanity seems doomed. At the last moment the Martian machines come tumbling down as their occupants succumb to Earth's germs, since they lack immunity to combat these microscopic entities.

SCIENTIFIC COMMENTARY

Astronomy.   In the opening sequence we are given a tour of the solar system. The statement that Mars is inhabited by intelligent beings we now know to be false. The landers we placed on the surface of Mars

War of the Worlds: A Martian war machine wreaks havoc on Los Angeles. (Photo: Museum of Modern Art/Film Stills Archive. Courtesy of Paramount Pictures.)

have analyzed soil samples and reported that the soil lacks any form of life. Close-up photographic studies also show Mars to be a dead planet. It has no vegetation, nor are there artificial canals criss-crossing its surface.

Meteors.   The film correctly notes that a meteor the size of the first Martian vehicle would have made an immense crater unless it decelerated before hitting the ground or was hollow. Meteorites (meteors that reach the ground) are not hollow; rather they are metallic and/or solid rock. A meteor as large as the Martian vehicle would make a crater many times larger than that depicted. For example, a meteorite weighing at least 30,000 tons hit Arizona about 24,000 years ago. This Barringer crater is nearly 500 feet deep and 4,000 feet across.

Nuclear Explosions and Their Effects.   The atomic bomb dropped on a group of the Martian spaceships has no effect. This seems incredible since the temperature at the center of the fireball produced by the explosion of an atomic bomb is millions of degrees Fahrenheit. It might be possible to shield the Martian vehicles from charged particles, such as protons emitted by the explosion, by surrounding the vehicles with high magnetic fields, much as the Earth's magnetic field shields it from some cosmic rays that carry a net charge. However, this magnetic field would shield the occupants neither from deadly neutrons that have no electrical charge (they are the basis for the so-called neutron bomb) nor from x-rays and gamma-rays also emitted in the explosion, since these are bundles of electromagnetic energy that have no electrical charge. In short, the atomic bomb would have killed the Martians.

2001: A Space Odyssey

- MGM (USA), 1968, color, 139 minutes
- **Credits:** *Producer and director*, Stanley Kubrick; *screenplay*, Stanley Kubrick and Arthur C. Clarke, based on "The Sentinel," by Arthur C. Clarke; *cinematographers*, Geoffrey Unsworth and John Alcott; *special effects*, Douglas Trumbull
- **Cast:** Keir Dullea (Commander David Bowman), Gary Lockwood (Frank Poole), William Sylvester (Dr. Heywood Floyd), and Douglas Rain (voice of HAL)

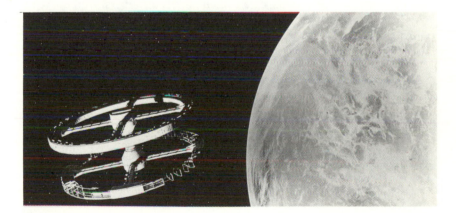

2001: The rotating space station in orbit about the Earth. (Photo: Museum of Modern Art/Film Stills Archive. Courtesy of Metro-Goldwyn-Mayer.)

PLOT SUMMARY

At the beginning of the film, a mysterious black monolith enhances the intelligence of our prehuman ancestors. Then the film jumps forward to the year 1999, when the human race has established permanent colonies on the Moon and also a permanent space station orbiting the Earth. An important scientific administrator, Dr. Heywood Floyd, is seen going to America's Moon base to investigate a mysterious monolith that has been found beneath the surface of the Moon. It has been buried for 5 million years. As it is being examined, it emits a signal aimed at Jupiter.

The next segment of the film takes place in 2001, aboard the spaceship *Discovery I*, which is traveling toward Jupiter. Three crew members are in suspended animation in order to conserve food and air, while two others pilot the ship with the help of a supercomputer named HAL. The computer goes berserk and kills four of the crew members before it is deactivated. The fifth astronaut, Commander Bowman, finally reaches Jupiter. A giant monolith is in orbit around the planet. As Bowman approaches the monolith, he is absorbed into some type of time-warp inside of the monolith, where the normal human life cycle seems to be tremendously accelerated. At the end, Bowman is transformed into a baby, which views the universe.

SCIENTIFIC COMMENTARY

Evolution.   In the opening sequence, the film attributes human intelligence to the intervention of an alien superrace several million years ago. This is contrary to accepted theory, well supported by many anthropological artifacts, that the human race, and our intelligence, evolved naturally and gradually over millions of years.

Space Travel.   The film correctly depicts travel in outer space. The occupants of a space shuttle to the revolving space station would feel weightless, as depicted in the film. The rotation of the space station could create the sensation of gravity, similar to the "pull" a merry-go-round rider experiences toward the rim of the merry-go-round (see Figure 11.1). The docking maneuvers are very well done.

Magnetism.   The buried monolith found on the Moon has a huge magnetic field associated with it. This magnetic field would be a way of determining when the human race had become technologically advanced — we would need both space travel and sensitive magnetic detec-

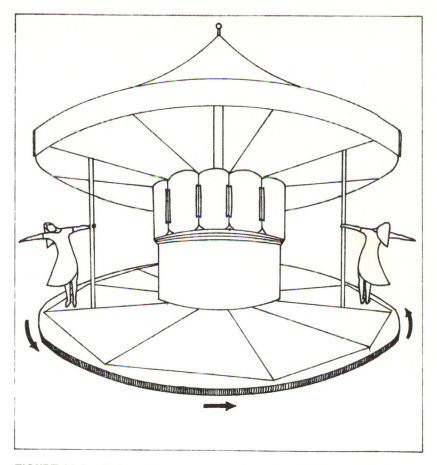

FIGURE 11.1.   Riders on a merry-go-round feel a "pull" towards the rim, which could be used to create "artificial" gravity on a rotating space station.

tors to locate the monolith, which promptly signals the giant monolith in orbit around Jupiter when intelligent beings reach it. But wouldn't it have been easier for the giant monolith (presumably a sophisticated robot left behind by a supercivilization) just to have monitored Earth for radio and television transmissions to determine when we became technologically advanced?

Space Travel.   The sequence in which Commander Bowman reenters the spacecraft without a helmet seems implausible. The shock of the extreme cold and zero atmosphere as well as his impact against the door of the entrance way would almost certainly have incapacitated him, making it impossible for him to close the airlock.

Computers. It is difficult to predict the characteristics of a computer with true artificial intelligence, since we presently cannot build any such device. Computers play chess, for example, by examining every possible move and reply. It is their great speed at doing this, as well as the sophistication of their programs for evaluating each final position, that has made them into formidable opponents for most human chess players. But their approach is fundamentally different than that of a human chess master, who dismisses all but a handful of moves as antipositional and does relatively little calculating compared to that of a chess-playing computer.

2010

- MGM (USA), 1984, color, 115 minutes
- **Credits:** *Producer, director, and screenplay*, Peter Hyams, based on *2010: Odyssey Two*, by Arthur C. Clarke; *special effects*, Richard Edlund; *music*, David Shire
- **Cast:** Roy Scheider (Dr. Heywood Floyd), John Lithgow (Walter Curnov), Helen Mirren (Tanya Orlova), Bob Balaban (R. Chandra), Keir Dullea (Commander David Bowman), and Douglas Rain (voice of HAL)

PLOT SUMMARY

Nine years after *2001*, a second expedition is sent to Jupiter to investigate the two-kilometer-long monolith that is circling the planet. The expedition is Russian, with 3 American scientists aboard who are to reactivate HAL and return to Earth on the American spaceship, *Discovery I*, which is still in orbit around Jupiter. They discover that HAL malfunctioned because of orders to lie about the real mission to the crew of the first expedition. The giant monolith turns out to be lethal to anyone approaching too closely. Finally, the second expedition is warned and departs before the monolith turns Jupiter into a second sun, which will warm the moon Europa, on which another life form is developing.

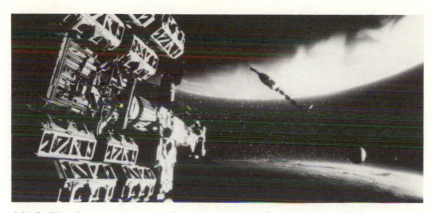

2010: The Russian spacecraft *Leonov* (left) is stationed close to the tumbling American spacecraft *Discovery*. Jupiter and one of its largest moons, Io, are seen in the distance. (Photo: Museum of Modern Art/Film Stills Archive. Courtesy of Metro-Goldwyn-Mayer.)

SCIENTIFIC COMMENTARY

Computers. The assertion in the film that the supercomputer, named HAL, went berserk because it was ordered to lie to the crew members of *Discovery I* about the true mission of the expedition to Jupiter is difficult to comment on scientifically. The psychological characteristics of an artificial intelligence will have to await the advent of artificial intelligence.

Astronomy. The changing orbit of *Discovery I* would have to be caused by its being subjected to a changing gravitational field. The film attributes this to the giant monolith, which is also in orbit near Jupiter. We know of no physical mechanism by which the gravitational field of any planet could be changed, since it depends exclusively on two parameters, the mass of the planet and the distance from the planet.

Later, when the monolith descends to the surface of Jupiter and changes it into a second sun, we also have no physical principle to explain what is happening. The mass of Jupiter (318 times the mass of Earth) is too small for it to become a sun. There is a minimum mass, about 30,000 times the mass of Earth, required in order for the internal gravitational attraction of a stellar object to produce sufficiently high pressures, and consequently temperatures of millions of degrees, to ignite the thermonuclear process at the center of the object. This process transforms four hydrogen nuclei into one helium nucleus, a process accompanied by the release of energy. The high temperature is needed to provide sufficient kinetic energy to the protons to overcome the electrical repulsion of their positive charges. Only when the protons are close together does the attractive, short-range, nuclear force form them into helium nuclei. This is the process that powers our Sun.

When Jupiter ignites into a new sun, the explosion and accompanying burst of radiation would have killed the occupants of the Russian spaceship and probably destroyed the ship itself. Furthermore, the ignition of the thermonuclear process, if it occurred due to the actions of the giant monolith, would have produced an outward pressure so great that Jupiter's gravitational field could not have held it together. Jupiter would have blown apart since it could not continue to exist as a stable sun.

Jupiter has a huge vortex, which is called the Great Red Spot. It measures about 9,000 miles by 25,000 miles and was first observed three centuries ago.

The glaring light that is seen when the door of the Soviet spaceship is opened for the astronauts to go to *Discovery I* is incorrect. At the much greater distance of Jupiter from the Sun, the light intensity would only be about 4% as great as at the upper atmosphere of the Earth.

Momentum.   We see the conservation of linear momentum depicted in the film as the Russian and American crewmen transfer from the Russian spaceship to *Discovery I*. The Russian crewman uses an oxygen tank as a propellant system: he fires the gas toward the Russian spaceship, and the two crewmen are moved toward the American spaceship. We also see the conservation of angular momentum in the constant rotation of part of the Soviet ship as well as of *Discovery I*. This rotation would simulate the effects of gravity in parts of each ship.

Biology.   The crew members are placed in some kind of deep sleep, perhaps like the hibernation of a bear, to conserve food and oxygen. This cannot be done at present.

Countdown

- Warner Brothers (USA), 1968, color, 101 minutes
- **Credits:** *Producer*, William Conrad; *director*, Robert Altman; *screenplay*, Loring Mandel, based on the story by Hank Searles; *cinematographer*, William W. Spencer; *music*, Leonard Rosenman

• **Cast:** James Caan (Lee Stegler), Robert Duval (Chiz Stewart), Joanna Moore (Mickey Stegler), and Barbara Baxley (Jean Stewart)

PLOT SUMMARY

At the beginning of the film, three Apollo astronauts have a training exercise cut short because the Russians have just launched an astronaut into orbit around the Moon. The Americans expect the Russians to attempt a lunar landing in about three weeks. We are to get there first by utilizing a contingency plan, code named "Pilgrim," which will send one astronaut alone to the surface of the Moon. He will find a survival chamber already rocketed to the Moon and live in the shelter until the first Apollo mission to the moon picks him up in 10 or 12 months. Additional supplies will be rocketed to him to keep him alive until then.

Although the space agency planned to send a military man (Col. Chiz Stewart) on this mission, when Washington officials learn that the Soviet spacecraft will be manned by scientists, they insist that our astronaut also be a nonmilitary type. Thus both the decision to launch this mission and the crew selection are determined solely in reaction to what the Soviets are doing. The space agency officials then persuade astronaut Lee Stegler to take a crash course to familiarize himself with the equipment and to undertake the seemingly suicidal mission. Much of the film describes the brutally hard training sessions. We also see what it is like to pilot one of these early spacecraft. Stegler lands on the Moon and discovers that all three of the Russians are dead. He finds the survival chamber just as his oxygen is used up.

SCIENTIFIC COMMENTARY

Political Science. Much of the film deals with politics taking precedence over science in the decision-making process. This is almost a precurser of the Challenger disaster, where meeting preset time schedules for launches seemingly took precedence over safety considerations.

Spaceships. The film vividly portrays the difficulty of seeing out of the small window on the spacecraft and the discomfort of living inside a cabin so small that movement is virtually impossible.

Engineering. We have a realistic glimpse of the complexities of the spacecraft and the difficulty faced by engineers at mission control in trying to determine the cause of its malfunction. The film includes malfunctions in the craft similar to those that the real Moon missions encountered.

Astronomy. The surface of the Moon is reasonably accurately portrayed, with perhaps the exception that the powdery regolith that covers the Moon is not evident. This surface was caused by the Moon's being bombarded by micrometeorites over billions of years.

Meteor

- American International (USA), 1979, color, 107 minutes
- **Credits:** *Producers*, Arnold Orgolini and Theodore Parvin; *director*, Ronald Neame; *screenplay*, Stanley Mann and Edward H. North, based on a story by North; *cinematographer*, Paul Lohmann; *special effects*, Glen Robinson and Robert Steaples; *music*, Lawrence Rosenthal
- **Cast:** Sean Connery (Paul Bradley), Natalie Wood (Tatiana), Karl Malden (Sherwood), Brian Keith (Dubov), and Martin Landau (General Adlon)

PLOT SUMMARY

The picture commences with an American scientist, Paul Bradley, being picked up by the Coast Guard in the middle of a sailboat race. He is told by space officials that a new comet had entered the solar system and collided with an asteroid 20 miles in diameter. The explosion has sent a piece of the asteroid 5 miles in diameter, plus some smaller "splinters," on a collision course with the Earth. The only hope of stopping this meteor from hitting the Earth is to intercept and destroy it, using a battery of nuclear missiles that are orbiting the planet on a space platform, code named "Hercules." Calculations indicate that the U.S. missiles are by themselves insufficient to destroy the meteor. The Russians have a similar space weapon whose missiles, combined with America's, can get the job done.

The film describes the steps needed to overcome opposition from both countries' military to using their ultimate weapons against the meteor—leaving each country without a space weapon to brandish against each other. Splinters strike near Hong Kong (causing a giant tidal wave) and New York City, nearly destroying the Hercules control center. The combined missiles of both countries do finally destroy the meteor and humanity is saved.

SCIENTIFIC COMMENTARY

Astronomy.   In the opening sequence the film accurately describes a comet and its orbit about the Sun. The asteroid belt is also depicted, as is the collision between the comet and the asteroid as seen from the first American mission to Mars, which is diverted to study the asteroid. The ship, *Challenger II*, is destroyed by the collision. All of this seems reasonably accurate.

The discussion of the destructive power of a huge meteor is accurate in some respects, but probably understates its impact as being equivalent to 2.5 billion tons of TNT. The volcanic eruption of Krakatoa in the last century is estimated to have been equivalent to 1.86 billion tons of TNT, and it had far less of an effect than that predicted for the meteor.

It is not clear why the missiles strike the meteor in waves rather than all at the same time. The latter would seem to be the best way to destroy it. However, some of the fragments of the 5-mile-in-diameter meteor would still likely hit the Earth, since the missiles are unlikely to vaporize the entire mass, as pictured. The effects of the two splinters that do strike the Earth seem realistic enough. The ability to plot the course of the main meteor is also realistic. It should be noted that some scientists think that the dinosaurs vanished as a consequence of a collision with an asteroid some 65 million years ago. The dirt thrown into the sky by that impact may have blocked the Sun's rays from reaching vegetation, causing the dinosaurs to starve.

Star Wars

- Twentieth Century Fox (USA), 1977, color, 121 minutes
- **Credits:** *Producer*, Gary Kurtz; *director and screenplay*, George Lucas; *cinematographer*, Gilbert Taylor; *special effects*, John Dykstra; *music*, John Williams
- **Cast:** Mark Hamill (Luke Skywalker), Harrison Ford (Han Solo), Carrie Fisher (Princess Leia), Alec Guiness (Obi-Wan Kenobi), and David Prowse (Darth Vader)

Star Wars: A rebel starfighter on its attack run against the Death Star. Note that all of its engines are exhausting out the rear of the craft only. (Photo: Museum of Modern Art/Film Stills Archive. Courtesy of 20th Century-Fox.)

PLOT SUMMARY

The film opens as a spaceship carrying Princess Leia is attacked by an Imperial warship. Two robots manage to escape with plans of the construction of the ultimate weapon, a huge fortified battle station called the Death Star, which can destroy an entire planet. The robots land on a remote planet where they fall into the hands of a farmer whose nephew, Luke Skywalker, discovers that one of the robots has a message for Obi-Wan Kenobi, one of the two remaining Jedi knights in the universe. Skywalker and Kenobi join forces to rescue the princess. They hire a mercenary pilot to fly them and the robots to the stronghold of a rebel uprising against the evil Empire. En route, they are intercepted by the Death Star. On it, they rescue the princess and escape with the robots. Rebel scientists then find a flaw in the defensive armaments of the Death Star, and Skywalker destroys it in the exciting conclusion of the first film in the *Star Wars* trilogy. The special effects were unprecedented at the time the film was released. The sets and futuristic equipment are spectacular.

SCIENTIFIC COMMENTARY

Astronomy.   The film takes place in a galaxy "far, far away," and thus little can be said about actual star systems. The film does predict traveling faster than the speed of light, a physical impossibility.

Energy.   The film repeatedly shows violations of the conservation of energy. The other Jedi knight, Darth Vader, nearly strangles a disbelieving Imperial officer using only his mind. Obviously the energy output of a mind is not nearly large enough to produce that effect, even if telekinesis were possible, which it is not. There are various allusions to the Force, a mystical power that only the Jedi knights have been able to harness with their minds. When Kenobi is struck down in a duel with Vader, his body is not to be found beneath his robes; it vanishes into thin air, once again a violation of the conservation of energy contained in the matter of his body.

Space Flight.   In the final battle scene in which the rebel starfighters attack the Death Star, we see the attacking space vehicles making banked turns. This is impossible in a vacuum such as outer space, since it is only the interaction of air on the wings of aircraft that permit banked turns. Further, we also hear the explosions that occur during the battle sequence. Once again, in the absence of air, sound waves could not be emitted from the explosions to nearby starfighters. In short, the pilots would hear nothing except the noises emanating from their own spaceships.

Robotics.   The two robots, R2D2 and C3PO, are given personalities and exhibit very human qualities such as loyalty and fear. This seems hard to understand in a robot, as does their constant bickering with each other.

Silent Running

- Universal Pictures (USA), 1972, color, 90 minutes
- **Credits:** *Producer*, Michael Gruskoff; *director*, Douglass Trumbull; *screenplay*, Deric Washburn, Michael Cimino, and Steve Bocho;

cinematographer, Charles F. Wheeler; *special effects*, Douglass Trumbull; *music*, Peter Schickele
    • **Cast:** Bruce Dern (Lowell), Cliff Potts (Wolf), Ron Rifkin (Barker), and Jesse Vint (Keenan)

PLOT SUMMARY

It is 2008, and the Earth is no longer capable of supporting vegetation. Specimens of many plants are kept alive in huge domed greenhouses attached to a fleet of space freighters. One of these freighters is near Saturn when the picture commences. Its crew of four humans and three robots receives orders to disengage the domes and then to destroy them with nuclear explosives. One of the crew members (Lowell), who had spent eight years caring for one set of domes, feels compelled to preserve at least one of them. He kills his three crew mates and feigns a crash into the rings of Saturn to mislead his superiors into thinking that the space freighter and greenhouse have been destroyed. The forest begins to die,

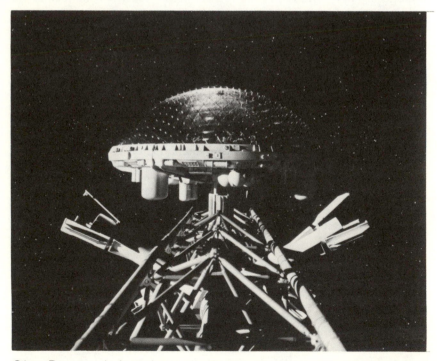

Silent Running: A domed greenhouse in outer space. (Photo: Museum of Modern Art/Film Stills Archive. Courtesy of Universal Pictures.)

and Lowell cannot discover the reason until he is contacted by a rescue ship, which notes that it is very dark at the location of the spaceship and greenhouse. Lowell then concludes that the forest needs more light! He sets up an array of lights in the forest and leaves the care of this facility in the "hands" of the one fully functional robot. He and the other remaining robot disengage the dome and then blow up themselves and the freighter.

SCIENTIFIC COMMENTARY

Astronomy.   The average radius of the orbit of the Earth about the Sun is 93 million miles, while the average radius of the orbit of Saturn is 887 million miles. Thus the intensity of sunlight at Saturn would, on average, be only about $(93/887)^2 = .01$ of the intensity of sunlight at the distance of the Earth from the Sun. Why would anyone carry a forest to a point where the sunlight would be insufficient to support the life of most plants for an extended period of time?

Energy.   The energy required to put any object into orbit about the Earth or any other planet is very large per unit of matter orbited since the escape velocity from Earth is about 25,000 miles per hour.

Engineering.   There is also the danger of a space garden being struck by meteorites. To minimize this danger, the domes would have to be made of transparent materials with higher tensile strength than any material now known.

Botany.   The motivation for establishing the orbiting greenhouses presumably stems from some serious limitation to the support of plant life on Earth. In order to live, plants require sources of carbon dioxide, water, nitrogen, phosphorus, sulfur, various other minerals, suitable temperature, and, of course, adequate light. Possibly one or more of these is absent or deficient. Another possibility is that some toxic condition exists on Earth that would kill the plants. Since the film appeared in 1972 when the dangers of pollution were becoming widely known, this may be presumed to be the cause of a barren Earth.

Black Hole

- Walt Disney (USA), 1979, color, 97 minutes
- **Credits:** *Producer*, Ron Miller; *director*, Gary Nelson; *screenplay*,

Jeb Rosenbrook and Bob Barbash; *cinematographer*, Frank Phillips; *special effects*, Peter Ellenshau; *music*, John Barry
   • **Cast:** Maximilian Schell (Dr. Hans Reinhardt), Anthony Perkins (Dr. Alex Durant), Robert Forster (Captain Dan Holland), Joseph Bottoms (Lt. Charles Pizer), Yvette Mimieux (Dr. Kate McCrae), and Ernest Borgnine (Harry Booth)

PLOT SUMMARY

It is 2130 and a spaceship approaches an apparent derelict ship, which turns out to be the spaceship *Cygnus*. It had been reported missing 20 years ago. It is now located very close to a giant black hole, which is pictured as a whirlpool in space. Upon landing on the *Cygnus*, the crew finds that the ship is not a derelict. Rather it is fully operational, manned by a crew of robots and hooded figures under the command of Dr. Hans Reinhardt, who had supervised its building and commanded it 20 years earlier. He claims that the crew, except for the father of one of his rescuers (Kate McCrae), abandoned ship 20 years ago after it was damaged. The crew apparently were all lost en route to Earth. The rescuers then learn to their horror that the hooded figures are the original crew members, now reduced to zombie-like individuals. McCrae's father was killed by Reinhardt. The rescuers and their robot, Vincent, then fight the robot guards of Reinhardt and the ominous superrobot, Maximilian. The robots are destroyed, but so is the *Cygnus*, which had used its power plant to maintain a stable orbit near to the black hole by nullifying gravity. The three surviving rescuers and Vincent get aboard a small probe, which then enters the black hole. They emerge unhurt from the other side of the black hole at the conclusion of the film.

SCIENTIFIC COMMENTARY

Astronomy.   The *Cygnus* could not have nullified gravity. Therefore it could not have maintained itself that close to a black hole, which has an immense gravitational field near it. Further, any spaceship pulled into a black hole would be crushed, killing all of its occupants. The scenes inside the black hole are pure fiction.
   When the ship starts to disintegrate, the air would have been lost throughout the parts of the vessel traversed by the fleeing rescuers, and they would have suffocated. Similarly, when one of them falls off the probe ship and starts falling into the black hole, he should have died from lack of air. Lastly, the propulsion system for Vincent to rescue him and

return to the probe is not clear. We do not see any rocket being fired in the direction opposite to which the robot moves.

Biology. We are told that the rescue ship, like the *Cygnus*, was seeking "habitable life" in outer space. Presumably this meant that they were seeking life forms. But why would they look near a black hole, which would pull into itself any object, living or nonliving?

Robotics. The two robots, Vincent and Maximilian, exhibit personalities and emotions that are inexplicable for robots. Nor is there any explanation as to how Maximilian was constructed by Dr. Reinhardt.

The Adventures of Buckaroo Banzai

- Twentieth Century Fox (USA), 1984, color, 103 minutes
- **Credits:** *Producers*, Neil Canton and W. D. Richter; *director*, W. D. Richter; *screenplay*, Earl MacRauch; *cinematographer*, Fred Koenekamp; *special effects*, Michael Fink; *music*, Michael Boddicker
- **Cast:** Peter Weller (Buckaroo Banzai), Jeff Goldblum (New Jersey), Lewis Smith (Perfect Tommy), Ellen Barkin (Penny Priddy), and John Lithgow (Dr. Emilio Lizardo)

PLOT SUMMARY

The picture commences with physicist–brain surgeon–rock star Buckaroo Banzai accelerating his jet car to 700 miles per hour. He then turns on a device called an oscillation overthruster, which so weakens the bonds between the nuclei and their electrons that his car can pass through an entire mountain of seemingly solid rock. He comes out the opposite side of the mountain with a tiny, alien life form in his jet car. He announces to the world that it came from the eighth dimension! At the news conference announcing his feat, aliens from this eighth dimension seize the overthruster and the scientist who had worked for decades with Buckaroo's father on the overthruster project.

Buckaroo follows the aliens and learns that they had been exiled from the eighth dimension. He is contacted by other aliens from the eighth dimension who are in orbit around the Earth. They warn Banzai that they will take any action necessary to prevent the exiles, led by the crazed Dr. Lizardo, from using the overthruster to return to their dimension, even if it means destroying the human race. Buckaroo and his well-armed friends finally destroy the villains and save the Earth. In gratitude for his efforts, the "friendly" alien spaceship even revives Banzai's friend, Penny Priddy, who had been killed by Lizardo's henchmen.

SCIENTIFIC COMMENTARY

Nuclear Physics, Atomic Structure.   The film states that the solid parts of any matter—the protons, neutrons, and electrons—comprise only one-quadrillionth (that is, one part in 10^{15}) of the space seemingly occupied by matter. This is a correct estimate and corresponds to the fraction of an atom that is occupied by the nucleus, which consists of closely packed protons and neutrons. Electrons move in a cloud around this nucleus, held to it by the electrical force of attraction between the positive charges of the protons in the nucleus and the negative charges of the electrons. Figure 11.2 depicts the electrical force lines between a

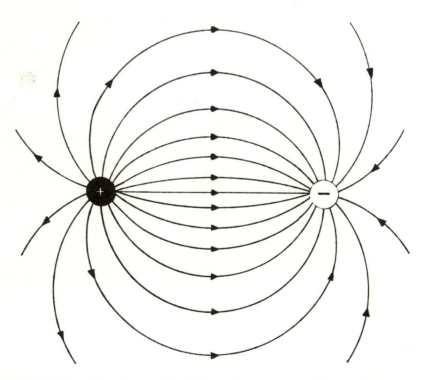

FIGURE 11.2.   The electrical field lines between a positive and negative charge.

positive charge (such as the nucleus) and a negative charge (such as an electron). As indicated below, the range (i.e., length) of these electromagnetic force lines is reduced by the overthruster. (See also the discussion of electrical forces in Chapter 5.)

The overthruster produces colliding beams of electrons and positrons, which, in turn, will produce quantities of elementary particles called intermediate vector bosons. These bosons, in turn, supposedly reduce the range of the electromagnetic force to less than the size of the nucleus. The jet car then passes right through space that is essentially empty, but it must travel swiftly to traverse the matter before it reverts to its original state. The energy released in the colliding beams could be lethal to anyone nearby. A paper was distributed at a 1984 scientific professional association meeting asserting that this was conceptually possible, although the hardware to produce these effects does not exist.

Alien invaders from the eighth dimension are, of course, fantasy.

Dr. Strangelove
Or: How I Learned to Stop Worrying and Love the Bomb

- Hawk Films (Great Britain), 1964, distributed by Columbia Pictures, color, 93 minutes
- **Credits:** *Producer and director*, Stanley Kubrick; *screenplay*, Stanley Kubrick, Peter George, and Terry Southern, based on *Red Alert*, by Peter George; *cinematographer*, Gilbert Taylor; *special effects*, Wally Veevers; *music*, Laurie Johnson
- **Cast:** Peter Sellers (Group Captain Lionel Mandrake, President Muffley, and Dr. Strangelove), George C. Scott (General Buck Turgidson), and Sterling Hayden (General Jack D. Ripper)

PLOT SUMMARY

The film begins as a right-wing Strategic Air Command general, on his own initiative, orders his planes to attack the Soviet Union. He seals the Air Force base so that there is no way for anyone to contact the attackers and countermand his orders. Further, a countermand would have to include a top-secret code number to be accepted by the attackers. The film alternates its episodes between the air base, the attacking planes, and the Pentagon War Room, where a distraught president tries to cope with the situation. There is biting satire throughout the film as the Americans are unable to recall their planes and they learn that the Russians have made operational a doomsday weapon that will automatically trigger enough thermonuclear devices to spread a lethal radioactive cloud over the entire planet. The system will be automatically triggered by any thermonuclear explosion on Russian soil. The film includes a Pentagon discussion of a possible mineshaft gap vis-à-vis the Russians, with mineshafts determining which country can better survive underground. The film ends as the doomsday device is activated.

Peter Sellers is superb, playing three roles, including that of Dr. Strangelove, a German scientist aiding the Americans whose Nazi mannerisms overcome him during the crisis.

SCIENTIFIC COMMENTARY

Communications.   The basis for the catastrophe depicted in the film is that the planes will only respond to a specially coded command coming from their home base. It is hard to believe that the fail-safe system that our Air Force was using at the time the picture was made would have had such a glaring defect in its recall procedure for American bombers.

Radar.   One attacking bomber is shown flying below the height at which the Russian radar can detect a plane, that is, very close to the ground. This was, in fact, a tactic that had been developed to foil an enemy's radar-controlled defenses.

Nuclear War.   The idea of a doomsday machine that will automatically and completely destroy all life on the surface of the planet seems preposterous, because precisely the kind of accident that the film describes would then. virtually destroy the human race. Some radioactive isotopes have much longer half-lives than those Dr. Strangelove is considering when he says that the human race will be able to emerge from deep mineshafts in only a hundred years.

Nuclear Explosion.   The film's depiction of a Russian defensive nuclear missile exploding only one mile from the incoming bomber without destroying it seems far-fetched. A missile with a one-megaton warhead would surely have knocked the plane down.

Crack in the World

- Paramount (USA), 1965, Technicolor, 96 minutes
- **Credits:** *Producers*, Bernard Glasser and Lester Sansom; *director* Andrew Marton; *screenplay*, Jon Manchip White and Julian Halevy;

cinematographer, Manuel Berenguer; *special effects*, Eugene Lourie and Alex Weldon; *music*, John Douglas

• **Cast:** Dana Andrews (Dr. Stephen Sorenson), Kieron Moore (Ted Rampion), and Janette Scott (Mrs. Maggie Sorenson)

PLOT SUMMARY

A team of scientists is trying to harness the virtually unlimited and untapped thermal energy inside the Earth. They are trying to drill through the Earth's crust to reach the molten mass within it (called the magma) and to bring it to the surface under controlled conditions. This would provide humanity with both a pollution-free source of energy as well as a source of metals. The project has reached a superhard layer beneath the surface, and conventional means fail to penetrate it. The project director, Dr. Stephen Sorenson, proposes to use a nuclear warhead to break through this last barrier between humanity and the magma. His assistant, Ted Rampion, opposes this because he fears that one more nuclear explosion, after all of the atomic tests, may fracture the Earth's crust. Sorenson, who is dying of cancer, persuades the authorities to approve the nuclear test. His laboratory is located somewhere in Africa, nearly two miles below the surface.

The test triggers massive earthquakes, and a crack in the crust starts to encircle the planet. A second nuclear explosion is then detonated to try to stop this crack, but it only causes it to accelerate and complete a much smaller circle on the Earth's surface. When this circle is complete, the "plug" of Earth above it is blown away to form a new moon, with the laboratory at the center of it. Rampion and Mrs. Sorenson barely escape.

SCIENTIFIC COMMENTARY

Geology. The film is correct in stating that the temperature rises as one descends into mines—about one degree Fahrenheit for each 60 feet below the surface.

The film shows a cross-sectional drawing of the Earth that is out of proportion to its actual cross-section. This drawing indicates that the project is trying to drill through the outer mantle to reach a completely molten inner mantle. The actual cross section of the Earth is depicted in Figure 11.3. Beneath the crust of only a few-miles thickness is a solid mantle of 1,800-mile thickness. Beneath that is a core of outer radius 2,200 miles thick: it consists of liquid metals with a solid metal inner core with an 800-mile radius due to the immense pressure.

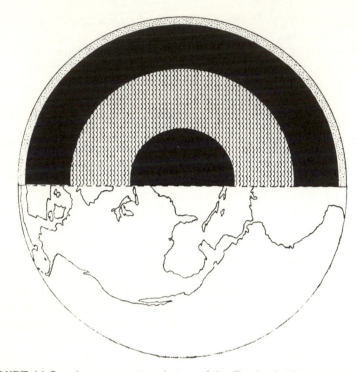

FIGURE 11.3.   A cross-sectional view of the Earth: the dotted outer region is the crust; the solid dark region immediately below it is the solid mantle; the light wavy region below that is the liquid metal core; the dark innermost region is the solid metal inner core.

The Earth does contain an immense store of thermal energy, and harnessing this energy would greatly alleviate future energy shortages. However, the Earth is so immense that any atomic explosion that did not destroy large surface areas by its detonation would be unlikely to cause serious earthquakes as an aftereffect. The explosion would certainly not cause a crack in the surface crust traveling completely around the girth of the planet. Furthermore, the pressure built up below the surface would never be great enough to blow away a huge chunk of earth at sufficient speed (5 to 7 miles per second) to go into orbit around the Earth as a new moon. Finally, if such an explosion did occur, it would be so large that Rampion and Mrs. Sorenson could never have walked to safety in a matter of minutes or hours.

The Time Machine

- MGM (USA), 1960, color, 103 minutes
- **Credits:** *Producer and director*, George Pal; *screenplay*, David Duncan based on the novel by H. G. Wells; *cinematographer*, Paul C. Vogel; *special effects*, Gene Warren and Wah Chang
- **Cast:** Rod Taylor (George, the time traveler), Alan Young (David Filby), Yvette Mimieux (Weena), and Sebastian Cabot (Dr. Hilliard)

PLOT SUMMARY

The film starts at the turn of the century, when an inventor tells his friends that he has found a way to travel through time. They do not believe him: he ventures forth in his time machine on his own. He visits London during World Wars I, II, and III and finally moves into the future to the year 802,701, where he becomes involved with a group of submissive humans called the Eloi and, in particular, with a young woman, Weena. The seemingly idyllic world in which they live is shattered for the time traveler when he learns that the Eloi are bred by a cannibalistic underworld race, the Morlocks. After stirring a revolt by the Eloi, the time traveler returns to the year 1900 to tell his friends of his journey and to select three books whose identities are withheld; he then returns to his true love in 802,701.

SCIENTIFIC COMMENTARY

Time Travel and Relativity. Time travel is not possible as depicted in the film, in which the time machine can move forward or backward in time. However, a kind of unidirectional time travel is possible. If an individual were in a spaceship moving at very close to the speed of light, all of his biological functions would dramatically slow down relative to an observer on the Earth. This result of Einstein's theory of relativity has led to the so-called twin paradox. This paradox involves two identical twins: one remains on Earth and the other travels at speeds close to light to a distant star and returns to find his twin brother dead for thousands of years. In this sense only, time travel may be possible. But the time traveler can never return to his original time period.

A second kind of "time machine," which can look backward in time, does exist. That "time machine" is the sky: the light reaching one's eyes has left the stars or galaxies in the sky hundreds, thousands, or even millions of years ago. One is therefore seeing these astronomical objects as they existed many years ago. In effect, one is looking backward in time. Our most powerful telescopes can detect light that has traveled billions of years to reach Earth. In effect, these telescopes are looking backward in time billions of years.

Biology and Sociology. The film reveals that the Eloi and Morlocks evolved in different ways from the human stock following a war lasting over three centuries. The Morlocks apparently retained some technological knowledge, since they are able to operate the underground machinery. Their eyes have become adapted to the dark and they were blinded by bright lights. Most cave-dwelling animals are colorless, but the Morlocks inexplicably have green skin.

Why would they have become cannibals when other food seems plentiful? It takes many years to raise a human being and an enormous investment in food for such human "livestock" as compared to other mammals. Since no other animals are shown, perhaps humans are the only surviving ones. Perhaps there was a time when no food but other humans was available for survival, and this circumstance led to the loss of the taboo against cannibalism. What other explanations can the class think of?

The Final Countdown

- United Artists (USA), 1980, color, 103 minutes
- **Credits:** *Producer*, Peter Vincent Douglas; *director*, Don Taylor; *screenplay*, Gerry Davis, Thomas Hunter, Peter Powell, and David Ambrose; *cinematographer*, Victor Kemper; *special effects*, Maurice Binder
- **Cast:** Kirk Douglas (Capt. Matthew Yelland), Martin Sheen (Warren Lasky), James Farentino (Commander Richard Owens), Katharine Ross (Laurel Scott), Ron O'Neal (Commander Dan Thurman), and Charles Durning (Senator Samuel Chapman)

PLOT SUMMARY

The departure of the aircraft carrier, the *Nimitz*, is delayed until a systems analyst, Warren Lasky, comes aboard at the request of the builder of this aircraft carrier. The *Nimitz* is engulfed by a gigantic time-warp and transported from 1980 to December 6, 1941, within striking distance of the Japanese fleet, which is about to attack Pearl Harbor. When the carrier's crew discover what has happened, they are faced with a dilemma: should they act and change history? The situation is complicated by the rescue of a United States senator, Samuel Chapman, and his aide, Laurel Scott, who have survived an attack on their boat by two Japanese fighter planes. The senator was the front-runner for the Democratic nomination for vice-president in 1944: Commander Owens, an amateur historian who is writing a book on the period, states that Senator Chapman disappeared on the day of the Pearl Harbor attack.

The *Nimitz*'s captain finally decides to attack the Japanese fleet. The time-warp then reappears and the ship and its aircraft are returned to 1980. However, Commander Owens remains stranded, by an accident which kills Senator Chapman, in 1941 with the senator's aide. At the end of the picture, this couple greets the returned Lasky: their company has built the *Nimitz*!

SCIENTIFIC COMMENTARY

Time Travel and Relativity.   See this section under *The Time Machine*.

Engineering.   The operation of the *Nimitz* is accurately portrayed.

Sociology.   Should the time travelers have tried to alter history? If they did so, might this have altered the future from which they had traveled? In a different future there might never exist an aircraft carrier called the *Nimitz*.

20,000 Leagues Under the Sea

- Walt Disney Productions (USA), 1954, color, 127 minutes
- **Credits:** *Producer*, Walt Disney Productions; *director*, Richard Fleischer; *screenplay*, Earl Felton, based on the novel by Jules Verne; *cinematographer*, Franz Planer; *special effects*, John Hench and Josh Meador; *music*, Paul Smith
- **Cast:** Kirk Douglas (Ned Land), James Mason (Captain Nemo), Paul Lukas (Professor Pierre Aronnax), and Peter Lorre (Conseil)

PLOT SUMMARY

The year is 1868. A scientist, Professor Aronnax, is asked to aid a naval vessel investigating a sea monster. On board he meets a master harpoonist, Ned Land. When they meet the sea monster, both the ship's guns and Land's harpoon are ineffective against it, and the warship is sunk. The professor, his assistant, and Land are rescued by the "monster," which turns out to be a submarine, the *Nautilus*, under the command of a Captain Nemo. The captain had fled an island prison with a group of inmates and had built the marvelous submarine. Its propulsion system is not described in detail, but the inference can be made that it has a nuclear engine. Nemo attacks and destroys warships and ships carrying munitions. His submarine is damaged during one encounter, and it sinks to depths lower than any human had ever reached. At these depths it is attacked by a giant squid. Land kills the squid and saves Nemo's life.

Earlier, Land had thrown overboard a number of bottles indicating the home base of Nemo. When the *Nautilus* arrives at this island refuge, there are several warships surrounding it and soldiers are swarming ashore. Nemo arrives at his base, located inside an atoll on the island, just ahead of the soldiers and sets off a massive explosion that destroys the island, but he is mortally wounded in the action. His crew decide to die with him by scuttling the *Nautilus*. The professor, his assistant, and Land just barely escape the sinking submarine.

SCIENTIFIC COMMENTARY

Engineering.   The submarine is huge in size and plush in its appointments. It is preposterous to suggest that a small band of escaped convicts could have constructed this marvel, which was far superior to any submarine in existence at that time. (Submarines were employed in the Civil War.)

Nuclear Physics.   Since the crew are never shown taking on board any fuel, such as coal or wood, during their extended voyage, and the explosion of the island is reminiscent of a nuclear bomb, the submarine's implied propulsion system is nuclear power—which was an impossibility in the 1860s. The theoretical foundations of nuclear power—that mass may be converted to energy—awaited Einstein's theory of relativity, which was first published in 1905.

Diving Equipment.   The scuba gear, including portable air tanks, was not in use until long after 1868. A diver would simply have had a hose supplying air from the ship.

Biology. Prof. Aronnax says to reporters, "If we could go deep enough, we'd all be surprised at the creatures down there." The "creature" terrorizing the South Seas turns out to be the *Nautilus*, but a deep-sea creature the voyagers encounter is the giant squid. So far no such giant squid is known to exist, but there have been extremely large squid beaks found in the stomachs of large whales. There are indeed many regions of the oceans that have not been explored. Occasionally there have been hints that the seas hold many secrets, such as the recognition of the supposedly extinct coelocanth, *Latimeria*, when fishermen collected specimens near Madagascar. Some progress in this area has been made in recent years because of the availability of small submarines capable of withstanding the tremendous pressures found at great depths. The research vessel *Alvin*, owned by the Woods Hole Oceanographic Institution, has allowed exploration, filming, and specimen collection from great depths. The volcanic vent regions visited by the *Alvin* were discovered to provide homes to animals hitherto unknown, including giant vent worms and "dandelions." But even the *Alvin* is unable to visit the deepest parts of the ocean, called the abyss. Remote probes have collected animals living in these regions of perpetual darkness, huge pressure, and extreme cold. Until recently these regions were considered to be devoid of life. Animals that live in regions of great pressure are very difficult to collect and study, for they neither live nor remain intact at pressures of only 1 atmosphere. Scientists have had great difficulty in examining the "dandelions" from the vent communities because of their fragility when brought to sea level. The giant squid in the film had no difficulty in coming from the depths to the surface of the ocean and fighting the crew of the *Nautilus*. It seems unlikely that this would be possible.

Westworld

- MGM (USA), 1973, color, 88 minutes
- **Credits:** *Producer*, Paul N. Lazarus, 3rd; *director and screenplay*, Michael Crichton; *cinematographer*, Gene Polito; *music*, Fred Karlin
- **Cast:** Richard Benjamin (Peter Martin), James Brolin (John Blane), and Yul Brynner (Gunslinger)

PLOT SUMMARY

"Westworld" is one of three gigantic theme parks; the others are "Romanworld" and "Medievalworld." For $1,000 a day, tourists may indulge their highest and lowest appetites. The three parks are staffed by robots, which are controlled by a human staff and computers. The robots seem human. They may be shot to death, befriended, and so forth by the tourists. They never strike back or interfere with the guests' pleasures. At night the injured or "dead" robots are removed and repaired for the next day.

Two old friends, Peter Martin and John Blane, arrive at Westworld and Martin soon "kills" the gunslinger. Suddenly, things begin to go wrong as an unidentified computer malfunction begins to spread like a plague throughout all three parks. The robots slaughter the guests: Blane is killed by the gunslinger, who then pursues Martin. Finally, the gunslinger is destroyed, but we do not know what caused the computer malfunction. Will this happen again?

SCIENTIFIC COMMENTARY

Robotics and Artificial Intelligence. This is the central theme of the film. At the outset the robots behave as one might expect, that is, they obey built-in prohibitions against injuring any human. There are also fail-safe mechanisms in the weapons used. For example, there is a heat-sensing device built into every revolver that prevents the gun from firing if it is pointed at a human being. Thus it is not clear how the robot can shoot Blane: its gun should not have fired when it was pointed at him.

There are excellent sequences in which the film shows the audience what the robot "sees" through its "eyes" and the advantages that the optical system of a robot might have over human eyes.

We are never shown precisely how the robots continue to operate once the human operators die; further, what is the power source for the robots? We see that some of them are deactivated after they run amok, presumably because they have exhausted their internal power supply. But why wouldn't they recharge the supply if they could act independently in other respects?

Engineering. The basic premise of the film, that guests could freely shoot up these robots for $1,000 a day, is preposterous. Surely the cost of building such robots would run into the hundreds of thousands or millions of dollars per robot. The concept of being able to repair them in a matter of minutes or hours, as depicted, is also far-fetched.

Sociology. Is it likely that such sophisticated robots would be used only in amusement parks? It seems more likely that they would be used primarily in industrial applications. After all, they would provide American industry with workers who never tire, never complain, and never strike.

Close Encounters of the Third Kind

- Columbia (USA), 1977, color, 135 minutes
- **Credits:** *Producer*, Julia and Michael Phillips; *director and screenplay*, Steven Spielberg; *special effects*, Douglas Trumbull; *music*, John Williams
- **Cast:** Richard Dreyfuss (Roy Neary), Francois Truffaut (Claude Lacombe), Melinda Dillon (Jillian Guiler), and Cary Guffey (Barry Guiler)

PLOT SUMMARY

The picture commences as a team of scientists headed by Claude Lacombe discover a flight of Navy planes that disappeared in 1945. The planes are in mint condition, but their pilots are still missing. The story then centers on an Indiana power company technician, Roy Neary, who encounters a UFO while trying to fix a power outage. This experience changes his life, as he gets a fixation for an oddly shaped object that eventually turns out to be Devil's Tower in Wyoming. Many people who have had a near encounter with a UFO are drawn there. Neary meets Jillian Guiler during his quest to identify the object; they finally reach Devil's Tower as the alien mother ship lands. It is immense in size. Many humans leave it; all are the same age as when they disappeared. Among them is Guiler's son, Barry. A number of humans depart voluntarily on the alien spaceship, including Neary, who seems oblivious of any responsibility to his own family. The aliens seem friendly and nonthreatening. The signal they use to contact the Earthlings is a musical tune. The film ends with a view of the inside of the immense spaceship.

SCIENTIFIC COMMENTARY

UFOs.   Dr. Allen Hynek, the U.S. Air Force scientific consultant on UFOs (unidentified flying objects), defined a close encounter of the third kind as one in which the observers saw the UFO within 500 feet or less and also saw that it contained inhabitants. The film frequently alludes to famous UFO sightings or related events. For example, the planes in Flight 19 disappeared in what was later labeled the Bermuda Triangle. There is no mystery as to their fate, however. It was a training mission in which the one experienced pilot became disoriented and flew into the Atlantic Ocean, thinking that he was approaching Florida rather than flying away from land. It was after dark when the fuel ran out: the planes crashed at sea killing all crew members.

The chase of UFOs by police cars actually occurred in one midwestern state, but the police in that case were chasing moving lights, rather than clearly delineated vehicles as seen in the film. The fixation for an oddly shaped object that looks like a mountain is pure fiction, as is the contact with aliens.

Time Travel.   The return of the flyers who disappeared in 1945 without their having aged is inexplicable. Their biological time clocks would slow down appreciably relative to time on Earth only if they were moving close to the speed of light. Clearly they were not doing that all of the time while on the alien spacecraft, since additional humans were added, requiring that the ship be close to Earth and moving relatively slowly for the transfer of humans to the mother ship to take place. The motives of the aliens in picking up these humans is also hard to fathom.

Hangar 18

- Schick Sunn Classic Production (USA), 1980, color, 93 minutes
- **Credits:** *Producer*, Charles E. Sellier; *director*, James L. Conway; *screenplay*, Steven Thornley, based on a story by Tom Chapman and James L. Conway; *cinematographer*, Paul Hipp; *special effects*, Harry Woolman
- **Cast:** Darren McGavin (Harry Forbes), Robert Vaughn (Gordon Cain), Gary Collins (Steve Bancroft), James Hampton (Lew Price)

PLOT SUMMARY

A rocket fired from an American orbiting space vehicle accidentally strikes an alien space ship. One astronaut is killed by the debris from the explosion. The alien spaceship then crashes and is moved into Hangar 18, at a remote Air Force base, for further study. The government attempts to cover up the existence of this alien spaceship because of a forthcoming presidential election in which the incumbent had ridiculed his challenger for believing in UFOs.

The surviving two astronauts, who are being blamed for the death of their colleague, try to solve the mystery. Government agents at first just follow them, but as they get close to finding the truth, these agents attempt to murder them. Several agents and one of the astronauts are killed. The remaining astronaut reaches Hangar 18, and the presidential aide who had ordered that the spaceship be kept under wraps until after the election now orders Hangar 18 to be destroyed by crashing a plane loaded with explosives into it. The spacecraft survives the explosion, as do a number of the researchers at Hangar 18, and the world is told about the discovery as the film ends.

Much of the film is devoted to entering and examining the spaceship and its alien occupants, both of whom were killed when the missile struck the craft because the impact broke a vial containing a poison, which then vaporized. The aliens are very similar to humans. The investigators learn to read the aliens' language and discover that they have been visiting Earth for thousands of years. They have mated with our ancestors, and we are their offspring. Furthermore, they are planning a landing en masse in the near future!

SCIENTIFIC COMMENTARY

Evolution.   We do not need to invoke mating of our ancestors with alien astronauts to account for our intelligence or for the achievements of ancient civilizations, such as the building of the Great Pyramid in Egypt. Furthermore, the likelihood of compatibility between the cells of two races that have evolved on two different planets is extremely small. In short, it is very unlikely that human women could have borne the babies fathered by the aliens, as described in the film.

Physics.   The spaceship is powered by a nuclear engine, yet the workers appear to be cavalier in their exposure to possible radiation when turning on the engines.

Biology.   The workers at Hangar 18 pick up and move the aliens with their bare hands. This exposed them to possible bacteria or viruses living on or in the aliens. Since humans might not have immunity to such organisms, medical officials would have mandated extreme care in handling the alien corpses.

The Thing

- RKO (USA), 1951, black and white, 87 minutes
- **Credits:** *Producer*, Howard Hawks; *director*, Christian Nyby; *screenplay*, Charles Kederer, based on *Who Goes There* by John Campbell; *cinematographer*, Russell Harlan; *special effects*, Donald Stewart; *music*, Dimitri Tiomkin
- **Cast:** Kenneth Tobey (Captain Patrick Hendry), Margaret Sheridan (Nikki), and Robert Cornthwaite (Dr. Carrington)

PLOT SUMMARY

A pilot is sent by the military to a remote outpost near the north pole, where he learns that the station's resident scientists had recorded the crash of an apparent spaceship the day before. Compass readings near the crash site are affected by the amount of metal in the ship. The area is also radioactive. When the military attempts to melt the ice in which the ship is embedded, an explosion occurs, apparently destroying the craft. The scientists then find an alien crew member, frozen in a block of ice near the crash site. They remove the block of ice and carry it back to their base, where one soldier accidentally melts the ice. The alien, who is alive, escapes.

Dogs tear off one of the alien's arms, and the scientists find from examination of the arm that it has similarities to plants and contains "no animal tissue." Dr. Carrington germinates seeds from a pod found in the arm, and they form pulsating, "breathing," immature aliens, which thrive on human blood plasma. The creature repeatedly attacks the humans, who are cut off from help by a fierce storm. They know that they are struggling for their own lives as well as the very survival of the human race. Unless they destroy the creature it will reproduce rapidly, and its offspring may destroy all of humanity. When it regenerates the lost arm, it proves a dangerous opponent. The scientists try to prevent its destruction in order to study it and try to communicate with it. They fail, and it continues to be hostile. Captain Hendry finally kills it with an electric current.

SCIENTIFIC COMMENTARY

Biology.   The humanoid form and the mobility of the alien creature are very unlikely plant behaviors unless the organism were a poor photosynthesizer and hence unable to get adequate metabolic benefit from light energy. While we never see the alien ingesting food, we must assume that its form dictates drinking blood through its mouth. This anatomic feature coincides with the basic animal body plan but is found in no organism that evolved in the plant lineage on Earth. In this case, since the alien evolved on a different planet, we can only assume that some similarities with earthly life occurred, such as cellular structure, but that other features of evolution diverged in ways that yielded body plans unknown on Earth.

The humanoid form of the alien leads the scientists to conclude that the alien has perished in the ice, since most earthly animals would have died. However, plants commonly survive at temperatures below the freezing temperature of water. Thus it is not surprising that the alien revives when the ice melts.

Another plant-like characteristic of the creature is its ability to regenerate body parts. The main difference between the regeneration depicted here and the common process in plants is that plants seldom duplicate the lost part exactly. Such fidelity is characteristic of animals instead of plants (e.g., the regeneration of a chameleon's tail).

The creature shows further similarity to plants in its formation of seed pods for reproduction. In plants on Earth, seeds are the product of the union of sex cells that takes place in a flower. There is no indication of a similar process in the alien.

Star Trek II: The Wrath of Khan

- Paramount Pictures (USA), 1982, color, 113 minutes
- **Credits:** *Producer*, Robert Sallin; *director*, Nicholas Meyer; *screenplay*, Jack B. Sowards; *cinematographer*, Gayne Rescher; *special effects*, Jim Veilleux and Ken Ralston
- **Cast:** William Shatner (Admiral James Kirk), Leonard Nimoy (Mr. Spock), DeForest Kelley (Dr. "Bones" McCoy), James Doohan (Scottie), George Takei (Mr. Sulu), Nichelle Nichols (Uhura), Walter Koenig (Ensign Chekov), Kirstie Alley (Lt. Saavik), Ricardo Montalban (Khan), Merritt Butrick (David Markus), and Bibi Besch (Carol Markus)

PLOT SUMMARY

The film is a sequel to a "Star Trek" television program, at the conclusion of which a late-twentieth-century despot, Khan, who was discovered in cryogenic hibernation on a spaceship, was left with 70 of his followers on an uninhabited planet. He had been the product of genetic engineering. In the film, the starship *Reliant* explores the planet for its use in an experiment to test the effects of the Genesis process. This process causes a matrix to spread out over an entire planet and changes the surface of the planet so that it can support life. Living things grow on its surface at an accelerated pace. But when the matrix is released, it destroys any life already on the planet, thus making it a weapon capable of destroying an entire civilization.

The *Reliant*'s crew are unaware of Khan's presence on the planet, and he and his followers manage to take over the starship. Khan then attempts to seize the Genesis formula from a remote space laboratory. The inventor of the formula, Dr. Carol Markus, was the former lover of Admiral James Kirk, whom she contacts for assistance. Kirk is surprised by the hostile crew aboard the *Reliant*, and Kirk's starship, the *Enterprise*, is badly damaged by the surprise attack. Nonetheless, Kirk manages finally to destroy Khan and all of his followers. However, Khan sets off the Genesis device; and in order to restore full power to the ship so that it can escape the spreading Genesis matrix, Spock, the Vulcan First Officer, sacrifices his own life. The *Enterprise* is saved and Spock is given a hero's funeral: his remains are rocketed to the newly re-created surface of a planet within the range of influence of the Genesis device.

SCIENTIFIC COMMENTARY

Chemistry.   There is no process by which the inert atoms all over the surface (and perhaps inside) of an entire planet can be changed readily into other atoms. Inert atoms by definition have an inherently stable structure, and they will not change into anything else in ordinary chemical reactions. Furthermore, reactions that change one element into another require large amounts of energy: to do this to an entire planet would require an enormous amount of energy. The extraordinary acceleration of all growth processes also seems impossible.

Mass to Energy.   The transporter used in the film to ferry personnel from a starship to a planet presumably changes each atom of the individual's body into electrical impulses that travel at the speed of light to their destination. How, then, can the starship personnel be transported *into* the core of a planet? Finally, travel exceeding the speed of light is impossible.

Phase IV

- Paramount Pictures (USA), 1973, color, 93 minutes
- **Credits:** *Producer*, Paul B. Radin; *director*, Saul Bass; *screenplay*, Mayo Simon; *cinematographers*, Dick Bush and Ken Middleham; *music*, Brian Gascoigne
- **Cast:** Nigel Davenport (Ernest Hubbs), Michael Murphy (James Lesko), and Lynne Frederick (Kendra Eldridge)

PLOT SUMMARY

At the outset of the film, an unknown heavenly body appears to pass between the Earth and the Moon. It seems to illuminate the Earth. This visible wavelength radiation, plus perhaps other forms of radiation that are invisible to the naked eye, changes ants into intelligent creatures and increases the scope of the activities they undertake. The ants also begin to cooperate with different species in addition to their own.

One scientist, Dr. Ernest Hubbs, suspects what is happening and wishes to undertake a controlled experiment to determine the level of intelligence of these modified creatures. He enlists the aid of James Lesko, a mathematician with expertise in information theory and cryptology. They establish their laboratory in the Arizona desert. When the ants attack the lab's generator, the scientists retaliate by spraying the area with a deadly yellow insecticide. It accidentally kills a resident elderly couple, while their granddaughter, Kendra, survives after taking refuge during the spraying. The ants next surround the laboratory with towers that reflect the sunlight and increase the temperature inside to levels that threaten the function of the equipment and the people. Lesko wants to continue efforts to communicate with the ants, but Hubbs prefers to try to destroy the organized activities of the colony by killing the queen. Meanwhile, believing that the ants want to punish her for killing some of them, Kendra wanders out of the lab. Hubbs, with an arm paralyzed and swollen from an ant bite, stumbles out to try to kill the queen, falls into a pit made by the ants, and is killed by them. Lesko finally believes that he must try to kill the queen and enters the colony with insecticide. He finds Kendra there and somehow mysteriously realizes that he and Kendra have been taken into the colony for some as yet unknown purpose.

SCIENTIFIC COMMENTARY

Biology. The film implies that the celestial events had some selective effects on the living things of our planet in such a way that only the ants were affected. This effect seems to be some sort of mutation that induces permanent changes in the ants' behavior. It is difficult to conceive of a mutation-inducing agent that would not also affect other organisms. Furthermore, most nonlethal mutations are single-gene alterations to the genetic information that seldom produce such sweeping and complex alterations in a species. Chromosomal mutations, involving large amounts of genetic information, tend to be lethal. In humans, fewer than 10% of embryos with chromosomal mutations survive.

The ability of the ants to adapt is depicted inaccurately when the ants are shown carrying to the queen a soil particle coated with the yellow insecticide. She eats the particle and starts to produce yellow eggs that develop into yellow, no longer black, ants that are resistant to the yellow insecticide. Mutational alterations cannot be made to order in response to changes in environmental conditions. Rather, preexisting resistance in the population would leave some ants alive, while susceptible ants would die. If none has the ability to survive, then the species would die out.

There is now tremendous interest in communication among social animal species other than other humans, and a great deal of scientific effort is devoted to studies of ants, bees, gorillas, whales, porpoises, and so forth. Discoveries of the intricacies of nonhuman animal communication are causing reevaluations of the sophistication and complexity in such communities. The fine line between instinct and intelligence has proven more difficult to pinpoint than originally envisioned.

The analytical skill of Lesko has not yet been realized by biologists or engineers. The amalgamation of biology and sociology has produced the new discipline of sociobiology, which is incompletely accepted by some and vigorously attacked and discredited by others. Sociobiology seeks to describe social practices of animals and determine the biologic roles and genetic bases of these behaviors. Thus today the film is less startling in its depiction of the modified ant communities than it must have been in 1973, when it was released. However, the communications among invertebrates thus far seem to be much more limited and programmed than the sort depicted in *Phase IV*. Neither is there any known ability of ants or other invertebrates to monitor human activities and thoughts.

Cosmic Monsters
(or the Strange World of Planet X)

• John Bash Productions (Great Britain), 1958, black and white, 75 minutes
  • **Credits:** *Producer*, George Maynard; *director*, Gilbert Dunn;

screenplay, Paul Ryder, based on *The Strange World of Planet X* by Rene Ray; *cinematographer*, Joe Amber; *special effects*, Anglo-Scottish Pictures; *music*, Robert Sharples
  • **Cast:** Forest Tucker (Gilbert Graham) and Gaby Andre (Michele)

PLOT SUMMARY

The film commences in a British research laboratory that is investigating the effects of very high magnetic fields on materials. The research is supported by the military in the hope that the effects might be used to so alter the properties of the metal in an enemy aircraft that it would disintegrate. A computer technician is injured in the laboratory, and a replacement, Michele, arrives. The laboratory is run by Dr. Laird, who becomes obsessed with his work. He is assisted by an American, Gilbert Graham.

An alien spaceship from planet X then lands: its occupant looks like a human being. He contacts Graham to warn him that the large magnetic fields being generated at the research station reach out for many miles and are creating a hole in the ionosphere, thus allowing cosmic rays to reach the Earth. The alien says that rays may cause insanity in humans and may also cause mutations in insects.

At the end of the film a horde of giant insects attack a rural schoolhouse; the alien's intervention averts disaster. The military are called in to deal with the insects. Finally, as the research project is about to be closed down, Dr. Laird becomes completely deranged and starts to turn up the magnetic field to its fullest power. In order to protect the entire country from being overrun by mutant insects, the alien destroys the research installation and Dr. Laird.

SCIENTIFIC COMMENTARY

Astronomy. There is no planet called X in our solar system, nor is there evidence of intelligent life on any planet in the solar system except Earth.

Magnetism. Magnetic fields can extend outward from a source for large distances, depending on the configuration of the source. It would be easy to determine the strength of the magnetic field at any point using a magnetometer. Thus the scientists would never have been in doubt about how far it extended. Magnetic fields do not cause a metal to change into a substance that crumbles when touched. Rather, a magnetic field only magnetizes certain materials, such as iron, in such a way that the material itself then functions as a magnet.

Energy. The claim that the magnetic field may build up even after the power is turned off violates conservation of energy, since the magnetic field has an energy content that is proportional to the square of the magnetic field. Hence a larger magnetic field requires more energy from some source; if the generator is disconnected there would be no source of the energy.

Biology. The claim that radiation (whether from nuclear fall-out or cosmic rays) can make insects grow larger is discussed in great detail in Chapter 6. Cosmic rays do not drive people insane.

The Fly

- 20th Century Fox (USA), 1958, color, 94 minutes
- **Credits:** *Producer and director*, Kurt Neumann; *screenplay*, James Clavell, based on "The Fly" by George Langelaan; *cinematographer*, Karl Struss; *special effects*, L. B. Abbott; *music*, Paul Sawtell
- **Cast:** Al Hedison (André), Patricia Owens (Helene), Vincent Price (François), and Herbert Marshall (Inspector Charas)

PLOT SUMMARY

The film commences as the wife of a scientist calls his brother, François, to say that she had killed her husband. His body is found crushed in a press in the factory owned by the two brothers. She is also searching for a fly, one with a white head. Police Inspector Charas takes charge of the case. He believes the woman to be insane. After first refusing to explain why she killed her husband, she finally agrees to tell the story when his brother claims to have found the fly.

Her husband, André, had discovered a way to disassemble an object into its constituent atoms and transmit them at the speed of light to a receiver that would reassemble them. Thus he could transmit any object or person to anywhere on the globe. After disassembling the atoms of the family cat and failing to reassemble them, he finally experimented on himself. However, a fly entered the chamber as he was being transmitted and he ended up with the head and arm of the fly, while the fly ended up with a human head and arm. This is the fly with the white head.

When she and her son failed to recapture the fly so that her husband could try to reassemble himself again, he begged her to assist him in killing himself. First, he destroyed all evidence of his work. Then he put his head inside the press and had her activate it. The inspector views this story as the fabrication of a deranged mind and is about to have her taken into custody when her son comes running in to say he has found the fly. It is in a spider web, with the small human head shouting for help as a large spider advances on the helpless fly. The inspector smashes both the fly and the spider with a rock, in the presence of François. Both men then invent the story that her husband committed suicide. Helene is a free woman at the end of the film.

SCIENTIFIC COMMENTARY

Conservation of Matter/Energy.   The film posits that the large human head has been transformed into a small head on a fly and vice versa. But where are the atoms from the human head that did not reappear in the small head of the fly? Note that the device cannot create something from nothing; it merely disintegrates and reassembles. But where did the reassembler get the additional atoms needed to create the much larger fly's head on André?

Speed of Light.   Matter with a non-zero mass cannot travel at the speed of light. Only light and other electromagnetic waves travel at the speed of light. The signal received by a television set is an electromagnetic wave, not a stream of electrons.

Biology.   André could not have two human brains at the same time, one in the fly's head, enabling him to think and write, and another miniature brain in the small human head on the fly. Further, why would the small human brain on the fly allow it to fly from the laboratory? It is also virtually impossible that parts of a fly could be integrated with parts of the human anatomy such that either creature would function.

Fantastic Voyage

- 20th Century Fox (USA), 1966, color, 100 minutes
- **Credits:** *Producer*, Saul David; *director*, Richard Fleischer; *screenplay*, Harry Kleiner, based on a story by Otto Klement and Jay Lewis Bixby, as adapted by David Duncan; *cinematographer*, Ernest

Laszlo; *special effects*, L. B. Abbott, Art Cruickshank, and Emil Kosa, Jr.; *music*, Leonard Rosenman

• **Cast:** Stephen Boyd (Grant), Raquel Welch (Cora Peterson), Edmund O'Brien (General Carter), Donald Pleasance (Dr. Michaels), and Arthur Kennedy (Dr. Duval)

PLOT SUMMARY

The film opens as a defecting scientist from behind the Iron Curtain arrives in the United States. Both superpowers have developed a miniaturization process for moving troops and equipment easily, but the objects return to their original size in 60 minutes. The defector brings with him the secret of how to maintain miniaturization for longer than 60 minutes. He is attacked before he can reveal his secret. The attack leaves him unconscious, with his life in peril from a blood clot in his brain. To save his life, the clot must be removed.

The military decide to miniaturize a submarine and send it into the scientist's circulatory system. A surgeon on board the submarine will then use a laser to destroy the clot. The surgeon's loyalty is in question and hence a secret agent, Grant, is sent along to watch him.

The miniaturized crew and submarine enter the body and destroy the clot despite the attempts of the real traitor, Dr. Michaels, to sabotage the effort. They lose the submarine to attacking white corpuscles, but all of the crew except Michaels manage to escape through an eye.

SCIENTIFIC COMMENTARY

Conservation of Mass/Energy. The miniaturization process would violate the conservation of energy, which states that energy cannot be created or destroyed but may only change its form. When the ship is miniaturized, where has most of the mass gone (mass is a form of energy)? Clearly the ship does not weigh several tons when it is inside the scientist's blood vessels or it would be pulled right through them by gravity. Nor can we assume that the miniaturization process draws away energy from objects as they grow smaller, because they spontaneously return to their original size and mass. Furthermore, the film states that nuclear fuel cannot be miniaturized. Yet all atoms (which the film says can be miniaturized) have at their centers a nucleus that consists of the same components as nuclear fuels — a contradiction. Finally, even if the

Fantastic Voyage: Two crew members return to the miniaturized submarine, which is located in a blood vessel. (Photo: Museum of Modern Art/Film Stills Archive. Courtesy of 20th Century-Fox.)

ship had been ingested by white corpuscles, its atoms would return to their original size at the end of 60 minutes, killing the scientist.

Biology.   While the microanatomic imagery of the film is in many respects correct and obviously inspired by identifiable anatomic features, there are numerous errors in the imagery. For example, the journey begins with the entry of the ship into the carotid artery, and the blood is shown with far too few cells. Blood volume is about half plasma (the fluid part) and half cells, so there should be as much volume in cells as in fluid. The most serious errors involve aspects of immune functions, particularly those involving antibodies. The antibodies are shown actively seeking out and attacking Miss Peterson, the ship, and Dr. Michaels. Antibodies are protein molecules that would not be visible to the adventurers, just as the proteins dissolved in the plasma are invisible. The antibody response takes days to develop, not minutes as shown, and when it does occur, the antibodies encounter their targets passively rather than actively. The antibodies themselves do not kill their targets but rather trigger other mechanisms of destruction. For example, an antibody-coated target is much more likely to be ingested by white blood cells than an uncoated target.

Dr. Michaels more than once states that the white blood cells will attack the ship if it starts to get larger, suggesting that size is the determinant for their ingestion process, which is called phagocytosis. This is incorrect, since blood phagocytes will attack particles of various sizes, living and nonliving.

Another serious error shows impulses of the nervous system whisking along as light. Nervous impulses travel as waves of shifting ion movement at the surface of neurons and do not move freely through the fluids between cells. When the end of a neuron is reached, the impulse is transmitted to another neuron by the release of a chemical that diffuses to another neuron and starts a new impulse on it.

Numerous other errors of anatomic detail are evident, and they will pose an interesting challenge to students to identify.

The Day of the Dolphin

- Avco Embassy (USA), 1973, color, 104 minutes
- **Credits:** *Producer*, Robert Relyea; *director*, Mike Nichols; *screenplay*, Buck Henry, based on *Un Animal doué de raison* by Robert Merle; *cinematographer*, William Fraker; *special effects*, Jim White; *trainer*, Peter Moss; *music*, Georges Delevue
- **Cast:** George C. Scott (Dr. Jake Terrell), Trish Van Devere (Maggie Terrell), Paul Sorvino (Curtis Mahoney), and Fritz Weaver (Harold Di-Milo)

PLOT SUMMARY

The film begins as Dr. Jake Terrell is completing a lecture about his work with dolphins at an island research center. He describes Alpha, the first dolphin born at the center four years earlier. We learn later that Dr. Terrell has taught Alpha to speak a number of words in English. Meanwhile a government agent posing as a writer manages to pressure the foundation funding the research to grant him access to the research center. Others in the foundation are also interested in the work, for more ominous reasons. They kidnap Alpha so they can use him to plant a bomb under the president's yacht to assassinate him. However, the naive and trusting dolphin is repeatedly lied to by the would-be assassins and told that "Pa," Jake Terrell, is in their boat. Finally, when "Pa" never appears, Alpha is so distraught that he swims home. Terrell then instructs him to stop the villains from using his companion dolphin, Beta, to place the bomb. Instead, Alpha plants the bomb under the killers' yacht and blows them up! At the end of the film, Dr. Terrell tells Alpha that he must not ever speak to humans again. They part with Alpha calling out "Pa" and "Ma," and then reluctantly swimming away.

SCIENTIFIC COMMENTARY

Animal Behavior. Communication within animal species is a well-known phenomenon, ranging from purely instinctual to fully learned forms. The complicated dances used by honey bees are inborn, instinctual forms of communication that are identical in different individuals. However, human conversation is a learned type of communication and varies from individual to individual. Most often, communication occurs between members of the same species, as in the previous examples. However, some very simple forms of interspecies communication can be recognized easily. A domestic pet such as a dog or cat is adept at communicating its need to eat or go outside. Experts currently disagree about what degree of more advanced communication is possible between the most intelligent animals and humans. The ability to use symbols for objects and actions is considered the most advanced form of communication. Humans readily learn to use words as symbols of objects and actions. Some investigators believe that some primates, gorillas and chimpanzees, have been able to master such symbolic communication and converse with humans. Others believe that the results remain equivocal and probably are due to conditioning. In any case, vocal communication between dolphin and human has not been achieved. While it is correct that aquatic mammals use complicated combinations of sounds to communicate with one another, so far humans cannot speak to dolphins in their language, nor can dolphins speak to humans.

Selected Bibliography of References and Criticism

TEACHING WITH SCIENCE FICTION

Using Films

Boutzer, Christo. "Science Fiction in the Classroom." *The UNESCO Courier* 37 (Nov. 1984): 22–25.

Burke, Michael C. "Free-Fall Sex and Golden Eggs." *Science Teacher* 45 (Mar. 1978): 33–34.

Dubeck, Leroy W. "Science and Science Fiction Films." *Journal of College Science Teaching* 11 (Nov. 1981): 111–13.

———, and Suzanne E. Moshier. "Teaching Facts with Fiction." *American Educator* 9 (Winter 1985): 41–46.

Greely, C. E. C. "*The War of the Worlds* in the Classroom." *The Wellsian*, No. 8 (1985): 27–28.

Maynard, Richard. "A Galaxy of Science Fiction Films." *Scholastic Teacher* 102 (Nov. 1973): 27–28.

Using Literature

Brice, William R. "Exploration of Space: Fact and Fiction." *Journal of College Science Teaching* 7 (1977): 107–10.

———. "Geology Teaching and Science Fiction." *Journal of Geological Education* 29 (1980): 105–7.

Calame, Gerald P. "Science in Science Fiction: A Seminar Course." *American Journal of Physics* 41 (1973): 184–87.

Freedman, Roger A., and W. A. Little. "Physics 13: Teaching Modern Physics Through Science Fiction." *American Journal of Physics* 48 (1980): 548–51.

Gross, Elizabeth H. "Science Fiction as a Factor in Science Education." *Science Education* 43 (Feb. 1959): 28–31.

Hopkins, Lee Bennett. "The Future Is Now: Science Fact and Fiction." *Teacher* 97 (Feb. 1980): 42–44.

Hunter, C. Bruce. "Science Fiction for Teachers." *Science Activities* 17 (Nov.–Dec. 1980): 9–12.

Isaacs, Leonard. *Darwin to Double Helix: The Biological Theme in Science Fiction*. London: Butterworths, 1977.

Kirman, Joseph H. "Teaching About Science, Technology and Society." *Historical and Social Science Teacher* 13 (Feb. 1977): 54–56.

Lamb, Janice E. "Space Biology: Bringing the Far Out into Focus." *Science Teacher* (Sept. 1976): 19–21.

Lamb, William G. *A Sourcebook for Secondary Environmental Education*. Austin, TX: University of Texas, Science Education Center, 1973.

Lamb, William, and Roland B. Bartholomew. "Science Fiction—A Unique Tool for Science Teachers." *Science Teacher* 42.3 (1975): 37–38.

McCreight, Cathryn. "Hardware." *Colloquy* 4 (May 1971): 46–47.

Marks, Gary H. "Teaching Biology with Science Fiction." *American Biology Teacher* 40 (1978): 275–79.

Mayhew, Paula C. "Science in Science Fiction Mini-Course." *Science Teacher* (April 1976): 36–37.

Myers, Alan. "Science Fiction in the Classroom." *Children's Literature in Education* 9 (Winter 1978): 182–87.

Nunan, E. E., and David Homer. "Science, Science Fiction, and a Radical Science Education." *Science-Fiction Studies* 8 (1981): 311–30.

Rabiega, William A. *Environmental Fiction for Pedagogic Purposes*. Exchange Bibliography 590. Monticello, IL: Council of Planning Librarians, 1974.

Russ, Joanna. "Communique from the Front: Teaching and the State of the Art." *Colloquy* 4 (May 1971): 28–31.

Schmidt, Stanley. "Science Fiction and the Science Teacher." *Teaching Science Fiction: Education for Tomorrow*. Ed. Jack Williamson. Philadelphia: Owlswick Press, 1980, pp. 110–20.

_____. "Science Fiction Courses: An Example and Some Alternatives." *American Journal of Physics* 41 (Sept. 1973): 1052–56.

_____. "SF in the Classroom: Science Fiction and the High School Teacher." *Extrapolation* 17 (1976): 141–50.

Tashlick, Phyllis. "Science Fiction: An Anthropological Approach." *English Journal* 64 (1975): 78–79.

Wallace, Dawn. "Finding the Common Ground." *English Journal* 69 (Feb. 1980): 37–41.

Warrick, Patricia S. "Science Fiction in a Computers & Society Course." *Teaching Science Fiction: Education for Tomorrow*. Ed. Jack Williamson. Philadelphia: Owlswick Press, 1980, pp. 121–36.

Weaver, Edward K., and Elfred Black. "The Relationship of Science Fiction Reading to Reasoning Abilities." *Science Education* 49 (April 1965): 293–96.

Woolever, John D. "Science Fiction for Science Students." *Science Education* 35 (Dec. 1951): 284–86.

Zander, Arlen R. "Science and Fiction: An Interdisciplinary Approach." *American Journal of Physics* 43.1 (1975): 9–12.

SCIENCE FICTION FILMS

Books

Amelio, Ralph J. *The Filmic Moment: An Approach to Teaching American Genre Film Through Extracts*. Dayton, OH: Pflaum, 1974.

_____. *Hal in the Classroom: Science Fiction Films*. Dayton, OH: Pflaum, 1974.

Anderson, Craig W. *Science Fiction Films of the Seventies*. Jefferson, NC: McFarland, 1985.

Annan, David. *Cinefantastic: Beyond the Dream Machine*. London: Lorrimer, 1974.

_____. *Robot: The Mechanical Monster*. New York: Bounty Books, 1976.

Asherman, Allan. *The Star Trek Compendium*. New York: Simon and Schuster, 1981; London: W. H. Allen, 1983.

Atkins, Thomas R., ed. *Science Fiction Films*. New York: Monarch Press, 1976.

Baxter, John. *Science Fiction in the Cinema*. The International Film Guide Series. Cranbury, NY: A. S. Barnes, 1970; New York: Paperback Library, 1970.

Brosnan, John. *Future Tense: The Cinema of Science Fiction*. New York: St. Martin's Press, 1979.

_____. *Movie Magic*. New York: St. Martin's Press, 1974.

Clarke, Arthur C. *2001 Revisited*. Audio Cassette. North Hollywood, CA: Center for Cassette Studies, 1975.

_____, and Peter Hyams. *The Odyssey File*. New York: Del Rey, 1984.

Finch, Christopher. *Special Effects: Creating Movie Magic*. New York: Abbeville Press, 1984.

Frank, Alan. *Sci-Fi Now: 10 Exciting Years of Science Fiction from "2001" to "Star Wars" and Beyond*. London: Octopus Books, 1978.

Gerani, Gary, and Paul H. Schulman. *Fantastic Television*. New York: Harmony, 1977.

Gifford, Denis. *Science Fiction Film*. London: Studio Vista–Dutton Pictureback, 1971.

Hardy, Phil. *The Film Encyclopedia: Science Fiction*. New York: William Morrow, 1984.

Johnson, William, ed. *Focus on the Science Fiction Film*. Englewood Cliffs, NJ: Prentice-Hall, 1972.

Lee, Walt. *Reference Guide to Fantastic Films: Science Fiction, Fantasy, and Horror*. 2 vols. Los Angeles: Chelsea-Lee Books, 1972–74.

Menville, Douglas, and R. Reginald. *Things to Come: An Illustrated History of the Science Fiction Film*. New York: Times Books, 1977.

Meyers, Richard. *SF-2: A Pictorial History of Science Fiction Films from "Rollerball" to "Return of the Jedi."* Secaucus, NJ: Citadel, 1984.

Parish, James Robert, and Michael R. Pitts. *The Great Science Fiction Pictures*. Metuchen, NJ: Scarecrow Press, 1977.

Peary, Danny, ed. *Omni's Screen Flights/Screen Fantasies: The Future According to Science Fiction Cinema*. Garden City, NY: Dolphin-Doubleday, 1984.

Pichard, Roy. *Science Fiction in the Movies: An A-Z*. London: Muller, 1978.

Pohl, Frederik, and Frederik Pohl IV. *Science Fiction: Studies in Film*. New York: Ace, 1981.

Pollock, Dale. *Skywalking: The Life and Films of George Lucas*. New York: Ballantine, 1984.

Robin, Doris, Lee Vibber, and Gracia Fay Ellwood. *In a Faraway Galaxy: A*

Literary Approach to a Film Saga. Pasadena, CA: Exchequer Press, 1984.

Rovin, Jeff. *From Jules Verne to "Star Trek."* New York: Drake, 1977.

———. *A Pictorial History of the Science Fiction Film*. Secaucus, NJ: Citadel, 1975.

Saleh, Dennis. *Science Fiction Gold: Film Classics of the 50s*. New York: Comma-McGraw Hill, 1979.

Slusser, George, and Eric S. Rabkin, eds. *Shadows of the Magic Lamp: Fantasy and Science Fiction in Film*. Alternatives Series. Carbondale: Southern Illinois University Press, 1985.

Sobchak, Vivian Carol. *The Limits of Infinity: The American Science Fiction Film 1970-75*. South Brunswick, NJ: A. S. Barnes, 1980.

———. *Screening Space: The American Science Fiction Film*. 2nd ed. New York: Ungar, 1987.

Steinbrunner, Chris, and Burt Goldblatt. *Cinema of the Fantastic*. New York: Saturday Review Press, 1972.

Strick, Philip. *Science Fiction Movies*. London: Octopus, 1976.

Turnbull, Gerry, ed. *A Star Trek Catalog*. New York: Ace, 1979.

Warren, Bill. *Keep Watching the Skies! American Science Fiction Movies of the Fifties: Volume One, 1950-1957*. Jefferson, NC: McFarland, 1982.

Willis, Donald C. *Horror and Science Fiction Films: A Checklist*. Metuchen, NJ: Scarecrow Press, 1972.

———. *Horror and Science Fiction Films III*. Metuchen, NJ: Scarecrow Press, 1984.

Wingrove, David, ed. *The Science Fiction Film Sourcebook*. London: Longman, 1985.

Articles

Amis, Kingsley. "Science Fiction: A Practical Nightmare." *Holiday* (Feb. 1965): 8.

Anderson, Poul. "The Worth of Words." *Algol* 11.2 (1974): 11–12.

Arnold, Francis. "Out of This World." *Sight and Sound* 8 (June 1963): 14–18.

Ascher, Marcia. "Computers in Science Fiction." *Harvard Business Review* 41 (Nov. 1963): 40.

Bernabeau, Ednita P. "Science Fiction: A New Mythos." *Psychoanalytical Quarterly* 26 (Oct. 1957): 527–35.

Burgess, Anthony. "On the Hopelessness of Turning Good Books Into Films." *New York Times*, 20 April 1975: D1.

Burmester, David. "Science Fiction in Film." *English Journal* 74 (April 1985): 90–92.

Buscombe, Edward. "The Idea of Genre in the American Cinema." *Screen* 2 (Mar.–April 1970): 33–45.

Collins, Richard. "Genre: A Reply to Ed Buscombe." *Screen* 2 (Aug.–Sept. 1970): 66–75.

Collins, Robert G. *"Star Wars*: The Pastiche of Myth and the Yearning for a Past Future." *Journal of Popular Culture* 11 (Summer 1977): 1–10.

Crowther, Bosley. "Outer Space Comes of Age." *Atlantic* 189 (Mar. 1952): 91–92.

Dean, Joan F. "Between *2001* and *Star Wars*." *Journal of Popular Film* 7 (1978): 32–41.

Dempelwolff, Richard F. "Backstage Magic for a Trip to Saturn." *Popular Mechanics* 127 (April 1967): 106–9.

Dervin, Daniel. "Primal Conditions and Conventions: The Genres of Comedy and Science Fiction." *Film/Psychology Review* 4 (1980): 115–47.

Dworkin, Martin S. "Atomic Operas." *Contemporary Review* 203 (Jan. 1963): 27–30.

"Fantastic Voyages in Films." *The UNESCO Courier* 37 (Nov. 1984): 26–29.

Farber, Stephen. "The End of the World, Tale 1." *American Film* 8 (1982): 61–63.

Glass, Fred. "Sign of the Times: The Computer as Character in *Tron, War Games*, and *Superman III*." *Film Quarterly* 38 (Winter 1984–85): 16–27.

Gordon, Andrew. "*The Empire Strikes Back*: Monsters from the Id." *Science-Fiction Studies* 7 (1980): 313–18.

––––––. "*Return of the Jedi*: The End of the Myth." *Film Criticism* 8 (Winter 1984): 45–54.

––––––. "*Star Wars*: A Myth for Our Time." *Literature/Film Quarterly* 6 (1978): 314–26.

Graham, Wendy. "Wisdom of the Great Bird: Gene Roddenberry." *Space Voyager*, No. 12 (1984): 55–57.

Grant, Allan. "When a Camera Gets Under the Skin." *Popular Photography* 59 (Oct. 1966): 118–19.

Gregory, Charles T. "The Pod Society Versus the Rugged Individualists." *The Journal of Popular Film* 1 (Winter 1972): 3–14.

Hauser, Frank. "Science Fiction Films." *International Film Annual*. Ed. William Whitebait. Garden City, NY: Doubleday, 1958, pp. 87–90.

Heldreth, Leonard. "Ray Harryhausen: Neglected Genius of Animation." *Fantasy Review*, No. 86 (1985): 13–14.

Higsshi, Sumiko. "Invasion of the Body Snatchers: Pods Then and Now." *Jump Cut*, No. 24–25 (1981): 3–4.

Hodgens, Richard. "A Brief Tragical History of the Science Fiction Film." *Film Quarterly* 13 (Winter 1959): 30–39; *SF: The Other Side of Realism*. Ed. Thomas D. Clareson. Bowling Green, OH: Bowling Green University Popular Press, 1971, pp. 248–62.

Houston, Penelope. "Glimpses of the Moon." *Sight and Sound* 22 (April–June 1953): 185–88.

Hulseberg, R. A. "Novels and Films: A Limited Inquiry." *Literature/Film Quarterly* 6 (Winter 1978): 57–65.

Kane, Joe. "Nuclear Films." *Take One* 2 (July–Aug. 1969): 9–11.

Kennedy, Harlan. "The Time Machine." *Film Comment* 20 (Jan.–Feb. 1984): 9–16.

Landrum, Larry N. "A Checklist of Materials about Science Fiction Films of the 1950's." *Journal of Popular Film* 1 (1972): 61–63.

––––––. "Science Fiction Film Criticism in the Seventies: A Selected Bibliography." *Journal of Popular Film* 6 (1978): 287–89.

Le Gacy, A. "*The Invasion of the Body Snatchers*: A Metaphor for the Fifties." *Literature/Film Quarterly* 6 (Summer 1978): 285–92.

Leggett, Paul. "Science Fiction Films: A Cast of Metaphysical Characters." *Christianity Today*, 21 Mar. 1980: 32–33.

Mancini, Marc. "The Future Isn't What It Used To Be." *Film Culture* 21 (May–June 1985): 11–15.

Messenger, J. R. "I Think I Liked the Book Better: Nineteen Novelists Look at the Film Version of Their Work." *Literature/Film Quarterly* 6 (Spring 1978): 125–34.

Ohlin, Peter. "The Dilemma of SF Film Criticism." *Science-Fiction Studies* 1 (1974): 287–90.

Pohl, Frederik, Stanley Kramer, and Philip Strick. "The Movie Prophets." *Omni* (Nov. 1984): 68–70 ff.

Rogers, Ivor. "Extrapolative Cinema." *Arts in Society* 6 (Summer–Fall 1969): 287–91.

Roth, Lane. "Bergsonian Comedy and the Human Machines in 'Star Wars.'" *Film Criticism* 4 (1980): 1–8.

_____. "The Rejection of Rationalism in Recent Science Fiction Films." *Philosophy in Context* 11 (1981): 42–55.

_____. "Teaching Science Fiction Film Genre: Theory, Form, and Theme." *Journal of English Teaching Techniques* 11 (1981): 42–56.

Rutter, Carol A. "Hollywood Astronomy: Science Fiction Films." *Astronomy* 12 (Mar. 1984): 24ff.

Ryall, Tom. "The Notion of Genre." *Screen* 2 (Mar.–April 1970): 22–23.

Siegal, Mark. "Toward an Aesthetics of Science Fiction Television." *Extrapolation* 25 (1984): 60–75.

Smith, Jeff. "Careening Through Kubrick's Space." *Chicago Review* 33 (Summer 1981): 72–74.

Sobchak, Vivian. "Genre Film: Myth, Ritual and Socio Drama." *Film/Culture: Explorations of Cinema in its Social Context*. Ed. Thomas Sare. Metuchen, NJ: Scarecrow Press, 1982, pp. 147–65.

Sontag, Susan. "The Imagination of Disaster." *Commentary* (Oct. 1965): 42–48.

Stacy, Paul. "Cinematic Thought." *Hartford Studies in Literature* 1 (1969): 124–30.

Steffen-Fluhr, Nancy. "Women and the Inner Game of Don Siegal's *Invasion of the Body Snatchers*." *Science-Fiction Studies* 11 (1984): 139–53.

Strick, Philip. "Future Movies, Part 1: A Passion for Mandroids." *Films & Filming*, No. 366 (1985): 7–10.

_____. "Future Movies, Part 3: Range-Riders of the Nuclear Plains." *Films & Filming*, No. 368 (1985): 7–9.

_____. "Future Movies, Part 4: The Poisoned Planet." *Films & Filming*, No. 369 (1985): 7–10.

_____. "Future Movies, Part 5: The Invaders!" *Films & Filming*, No. 370 (1985): 6–9.

_____. "Future Movies, Part 6: The Utopian Paradox." *Films & Filming*, No. 371 (1985): 6–9.

_____, and Penelope Houston. "Interview with Stanley Kubrick." *Sight and Sound* 41 (Spring 1972): 62–66.

Tadros, Connie. "Film, TV and the Nuclear Apocalypse: Peter Watkins on Media." *Cinema Canada*, No. 111 (1984): 19–24.

Tarratt, Margaret. "Monsters from the Id." *Films & Filming* 17 (Dec. 1970–Jan. 1971): 38–42, 40–42.

Van Horne, Harriet. "Space-Rocket Kick." *Theatre Arts* 35 (Dec. 1951): 40–41.

Weinberg, H. G. "Novel into Film." *Literature/Film Quarterly* 1 (Spring 1973): 99–102.

Wood, Denis. "The Empire's New Clothes." *Film Quarterly* 34 (Spring 1981): 10–16.

_____. "The Stars in Our Hearts: A Critical Commentary on George Lucas' *Star Wars*." *Journal of Popular Film* 6 (1978): 262–79.

Wood, M. "Kiss Tomorrow Hello." *American Film* 2 (April 1977): 14–17.

Zito, S. "George Lucas Goes Far Out." *American Film* 2 (April 1977): 8–13.

Zwick, Doug. "The Genre Syndrome." *Jump Cut*, No. 22 (1980): 5–6.

SCIENCE FICTION LITERATURE

Books

Aldiss, Brian, and David Wingrove. *Trillion Year Spree: The History of Science Fiction*. New York: Atheneum, 1986.

Ash, Brian. *The Visual Encyclopedia of Science Fiction*. New York: Harmony Books, 1977.

Barron, Neil, ed. *Anatomy of Wonder: A Critical Guide to Science Fiction*. 2nd ed. New York: R. R. Bowker, 1981.

Bergonzi, Bernard. *The Early H. G. Wells: A Study of the Scientific Romances*. Toronto: University of Toronto Press, 1961.

Bova, Ben. *Through Eyes of Wonder: Science Fiction and Science*. Reading, MA: Addison-Wesley, 1975.

Bretnor, Reginald. *The Craft of Science Fiction*. New York: Harper & Row, 1976.

_____. *Science Fiction: Today and Tomorrow*. New York: Harper & Row, 1974.

Clareson, Thomas D. *Science Fiction Criticism: An Annotated Checklist*. Kent, OH: Kent State University Press, 1972.

Clarke, Arthur C., ed. *Time Probe: The Sciences in Science Fiction*. New York: Delacorte Press, 1966.

Clarke, I. F. *The Tale of the Future from the Beginning to the Present Day: An Annotated Bibliography*. . . . 3rd ed. London: The Library Association, 1978.

Day, Bradford M. *The Checklist of Fantastic Literature in Paperbound Books*. New York: Science-Fiction and Fantasy Publishers, 1965; New York: Arno Press, 1975.

_____. *The Supplemental Checklist of Fantastic Literature*. New York: Science-Fiction and Fantasy Publishers, 1963; New York: Arno Press, 1975.

Del Rey, Lester. *The World of Science Fiction 1926–1976: The History of a Subculture*. New York: Ballantine, 1979.

Dunn, Thomas P., and Richard D. Ehrlich, eds. *The Mechanical God: Machines in Science Fiction*. Contributions to the Study of Science Fiction and Fantasy 1. Westport, CT: Greenwood Press, 1982.

Ehrlich, Richard D., and Thomas P. Dunn, eds. *Clockwork Worlds: Mechanized Environments in SF*. Contributions to the Study of Science Fiction and Fantasy 7. Westport, CT: Greenwood Press, 1983.

Goswami, Amit, and Maggie Goswami. *The Cosmic Dancers: Exploring the Science in Science Fiction*. New York: Harper & Row, 1983; New York: McGraw-Hill, 1985.

Green, Roger Lancelyn. *Into Other Worlds: Space-Flight in Fiction, from Lucian to Lewis*. London: Abelard-Schuman, 1958; New York: Arno Press, 1975.

Gunn, James. *Alternate Worlds: The Illustrated History of Science Fiction*. Englewood Cliffs, NJ: Prentice-Hall, 1975.

Hillegas, Mark. *The Future as Nightmare: H. G. Wells and the Anti-Utopians*. Carbondale: Southern Illinois University Press, 1974.

Huxley, Aldous. *Literature and Science*. New York: Harper & Row, 1961.

Magill, Frank N., ed. *Survey of Science Fiction Literature: Five Hundred 2,000-Word Essay Reviews of World Famous Science Fiction Novels with 2,500 Bibliographical References*. Englewood Cliffs, NJ: Salem, 1979.

Nicholls, Peter, ed. *The Science Fiction Encyclopedia*. Garden City, NY: Doubleday, 1979.

_____, and David Langford, eds. *The Science in Science Fiction*. New York: Knopf, 1982.

Nicolson, Marjorie. *Science and Imagination*. Ithaca, NY: Cornell University Press, Great Seal Books, 1956.

Parker, Helen N. *Biological Themes in Modern Science Fiction*. Ann Arbor: UMI Research Press, 1984.

Parrinder, Patrick. *Science Fiction: A Critical Guide*. New York: Longman, 1979.

_____. *Science Fiction: Its Criticism and Teaching*. New York: Methuen, 1980.

Porush, David. *The Soft Machine: Cybernetic Fiction*. New York: Methuen, 1985.

Rasmussen, Richard Michael. *The UFO Literature: A Comprehensive Annotated Bibliography of Works in English*. Jefferson, NC: McFarland, 1985.

Reichardt, Jasia. *Robots: Fact, Fiction, and Prediction*. New York: Viking, 1978.

Sargent, Pamela. *Bio-Futures*. New York: Vintage, 1976.

Scholes, Robert. *Structural Fabulation: An Essay on the Fiction of the Future*. Notre Dame: University of Notre Dame Press, 1975.

_____, and Eric S. Rabkin. *Science Fiction: History, Science, Vision*. New York: Oxford University Press, 1977.

Silverberg, Robert. *Drug Themes in Science Fiction*. Rockville, MD: National Institute on Drug Abuse, 1974.

Smith, Curtis C., ed. *Twentieth-Century Science-Fiction Writers*. New York: St. Martin's Press, 1981.

Tuck, Donald H. *The Science Fiction and Fantasy Encyclopedia*. 3 vols. Chicago: Advent, 1972–82.

Tymn, Marshall B. *American Fantasy and Science Fiction: Toward a Bibliography of Works Published in the United States, 1948-1973*. West Linn, OR: FAX Collector's Editions, 1979.

———. *The Science Fiction Reference Book: A Comprehensive Handbook and Guide to the History, Literature, Scholarship, and Related Activities of the Science Fiction and Fantasy Fields*. Mercer Island, WA: Starmont House, 1981.

———, ed. *The Year's Scholarship in Science Fiction, Fantasy, and Horror Literature: 1980*. Kent, OH: Kent State University Press, 1983.

———, ed. *The Year's Scholarship in Science Fiction, Fantasy, and Horror Literature: 1981*. Kent, OH: Kent State University Press, 1984.

———, ed. *The Year's Scholarship in Science Fiction, Fantasy, and Horror Literature: 1982*. Kent, OH: Kent State University Press, 1985.

Tymn, Marshall B., and Roger C. Schlobin. *The Year's Scholarship in Science Fiction and Fantasy: 1972-1975*. Kent, OH: Kent State University Press, 1979.

———. *The Year's Scholarship in Science Fiction and Fantasy: 1976-1979*. Kent, OH: Kent State University Press, 1982.

Tymn, Marshall B., Roger C. Schlobin, and L. W. Currey. *A Research Guide to Science Fiction Studies: An Annotated Checklist of Primary and Secondary Sources for Fantasy and Science Fiction*. New York: Garland, 1977.

Warrick, Patricia S. *The Cybernetic Imagination in Science Fiction*. Cambridge, MA: MIT Press, 1980.

Weber, Ronald. *Seeing Earth: Literary Responses to Space Exploration*. Athens: Ohio University Press, 1985.

Wendland, Albert. *Science, Myth, and the Fictional Creation of Alien Worlds*. Studies in Speculative Fiction, No. 12. Ann Arbor, MI: UMI Research Press, 1984.

Wolf, Gary K. *The Known and the Unknown: The Iconography of Science Fiction*. Kent, OH: Kent State University Press, 1979.

Articles

Armytage, W. H. G. "Extrapolation and Exegetes of Evolution." *Extrapolation* 7 (Dec. 1965): 2017.

Ascher, Maria. "Computers in Science Fiction." *Harvard Business Review* 41 (Nov.–Dec. 1963): 40–42.

———. "Computers in Science Fiction—II." *Computers and Automation* 22 (Nov. 1973): 20–23.

Benford, Gregory. "Is There a Technological Fix for the Human Condition?" *Vector*, No. 119 (1984): 5–15.

Berger, Albert I. "Nuclear Energy: Science Fiction's Metaphor of Power." *Science-Fiction Studies* 6 (1979): 121–28.

———. "Science-Fiction Critiques of the American Space Program, 1945-1958." *Science-Fiction Studies* 5 (1978): 99–109.

Brians, Paul. "Nuclear War in Science Fiction, 1945-57." *Science-Fiction Studies* 11 (1984): 253–63.

Butrym, Alexander J. "For Suffering Humanity: The Ethics of Science in Science Fiction." *The Transcendent Adventure*. Ed. Robert Reilly. Westport, CT: Greenwood Press, 1985, pp. 55–70.

Byrd, Donald. "Science Fiction's Intelligent Computers." *Byte* 6 (Sept. 1981): 200 ff.

Clemmer, Richard O. "Mythic Process, Evolution, and Science Fiction." *Bulletin of the Science Fiction Writers of America* 13 (1978): 19–25, 29.

Conklin, Groff. "Science in Science Fiction." *Science Illustrated* 1 (July 1946): 44–45, 109.

Culles, Tara Elizabeth. "Science and Literature in the Twentieth Century." *Canadian Literature* 96 (Spring 1983): 87–101.

Franklin, H. Bruce. "Science Fiction as an Index to Popular Attitudes Toward Science: A Danger, Some Problems, and Two Possible Solutions." *Extrapolation* 6 (May 1965): 23–31.

Gallagher, Edward J. "The Image of the Scientist in Popular Culture." *Proceedings of the Pennsylvania Academy of Science* 53 (1979): 29–33.

Gopnik, I., and A. Gopnik. "A Brief and Biased Guide to the Philosophy of Science for Students of Science Fiction." *Science-Fiction Studies* 7 (1980): 200–206.

Goswami, Amit. "Science and Science Fiction: Co-Explorers of Reality." *The UNESCO Courier* 37 (Nov. 1984): 4–7.

Hirsch, Walter. "The Image of the Scientist in Science Fiction." *American Journal of Sociology* 43 (Mar. 1958): 506–12.

Hopkins, D. F. "Impacts of Literary Science." *Chemistry and Industry* 16 (Mar. 1963): 440–42.

Kincaid, Paul. "Science and Science Fiction." *Vector*, No. 119 (1984): 16–18.

La Faille, Eugene. "Computers in Science Fiction." *Voice of Youth Advocates* 8 (June 1985): 103–6.

Lear, John. "Let's Put Some Science in Science Fiction." *Popular Science Monthly* 165 (Aug. 1964): 135–37, 244–48.

Lem, Stanislaw. "Cosmology and Science Fiction." Trans. Franz Rottensteiner. *Science-Fiction Studies* 4 (1977): 107–10.

McCutcheon, Kathy. "Science and Fantasy in Science Fiction." *Vector*, No. 104 (1981): 7–13.

Medd, H. J. "The Scientist in Fiction." *Ontario Library Review* 46 (May 1962): 81–83.

Omer, J. B. "Manacle-Forged Minds: Two Images of the Computer in Science Fiction." *Diogenes*, No. 85 (1974): 47–61.

Pierce, John R. "Science and Literature." *Science* 20 (April 1951): 431–34.

Plank, Robert. "Quixote's Mills: The Man-Machine Encounter in SF." *Science-Fiction Studies* 1 (1973): 68–78.

"Relations of Literature and Science: A Bibliography of Scholarship, 1973–1974." *Clio* 5.1 (1975): 78–96.

Schatzberg, Walter, ed. "Relations of Literature and Science: A Bibliography of Scholarship, 1974–1975." *Clio* 6 (1976): 71–88.

――――. "Relations of Literature and Science: A Bibliography of Scholarship, 1975–1976." *Clio* 7 (1977): 135–55.

_____. "Relations of Literature and Science: A Bibliography of Scholarship, 1976–77." *Clio* 8 (1978): 97–116.

"Science Fiction Presents Strange Picture of Science." *Science Newsletter* 73, 10 May 1958: 296.

"Science in Science Fiction." *Advancement of Science* 26 (Aug. 1965): 195–207.

Stableford, Brian. "Man-Made Catastrophes in SF." *Foundation*, No. 22 (1981): 56–85.

Tymn, Marshall B. "The Year's Scholarship in Science Fiction, Fantasy, and Horror Literature: 1983." *Extrapolation* 26 (1985): 85–142.

_____. "The Year's Scholarship in Science Fiction, Fantasy, and Horror Literature: 1984." *Extrapolation* 26 (1985): 316–77.

_____. "The Year's Scholarship in Science Fiction, Fantasy, and Horror Literature: 1985." *Extrapolation* 27 (1986): 123–73.

Walsh, Chad. "Attitudes Toward Science in the Modern 'Inverted Utopia.'" *Extrapolation* 2 (May 1961): 23–26.

West, Robert H. "Science Fiction and Its Ideas." *Georgia Review* 15 (Fall 1961): 276–80.

Williams, W. T. "Science in Science Fiction: Alien Biology." *Listener*, 24 Dec. 1964: 1003–4.

Wright, James W. "TV's *Star Trek*: How to Mix Science Fact with Science Fiction." *Popular Science Monthly* 161 (Dec. 1967): 72–74.

Index

About the Authors

LEROY W. DUBECK is a Professor of Physics at Temple University in Philadelphia, Pennsylvania. He received his Ph.D. in physics from Rutgers University in 1965. He has taught an introductory-level physics course, "Science, Science Fiction and Film," at Temple University each year since 1977. The National Science Foundation has supported his innovative use of science fiction films to teach science, at both the college and precollege levels, with four grants over the past decade. He is the author of two other books.

SUZANNE MOSHIER is a Professor of Biology at the University of Nebraska at Omaha. Her experience in teaching many subjects prepared her for analysis of the diverse subjects of science fiction films. She has been collaborating with Leroy Dubeck on the development of teaching methodologies utilizing science fiction films since 1984 and with Judy Boss since 1986.

JUDITH E. BOSS received her Ph.D. in seventeenth-century British literature from Texas Christian University in 1971 and joined the University of Nebraska at Omaha in 1976, where she is now a Professor of English. She has been reading science fiction for over 35 years, teaching it at UNO for nearly 10 years, and has published articles on science fiction in *The Dictionary of Literary Biography, Extrapolation, Science-Fiction Studies*, and *The New Encyclopedia of Science Fiction*.